The Challenge of Conservatism

The Challenge of Conservatism

ITS ROLE IN THE
COMING HEAD-ON COLLISION

Paul A. Sexson
and
Stephen B. Miles, Jr.

Introduction by M. Stanton Evans

EXPOSITION PRESS　　　　NEW YORK

EXPOSITION PRESS INC.
386 Park Avenue South   New York, N. Y.

FIRST EDITION

Manufactured in the United States of America.

DESIGNED BY AMJAD N. QURESHI

EP 42093

To our children
Paul Alexander Sexson II
Timothy James Sexson
Elizabeth Fearnley Miles
Cheryl Louise Miles
whose futures we hope will be molded
by the philosophy this book expresses.

Preface

In January, 1964, Senator Barry Goldwater, announcing his candidacy for the presidency of the United States, pointed out the necessity for a "clear choice" between liberals and conservatives. This book seeks to outline the difference between the two. More than half the voters consider themselves either one or the other; studies have shown very clear lines of demarcation between the two; and the attitudes of liberals and conservatives on almost all questions—political, economic, religious, and personal —are amazingly consistent.

Gilbert and Sullivan were almost literally correct when they said:

Every boy and every gal that's born into the world alive
Is either a little Liberal or else a little Conservative.

This book was also written to point out *why* some are conservatives and some liberals, and to subject these philosophies of life to more searching scrutiny than they usually receive. It has turned out to be a conservative book. The basic reason, of course, is that the writers are conservatives, writing in an election year. But an important additional reason is that only from a basically conservative point of view can the full extent of the difference between liberalism and conservatism be made clear. Liberals tend to minimize this difference. Wherever they look, liberals are most impressed by likenesses, and often overlook differences—especially head-on collisions. Conservatives are inclined to concentrate on the unlikenesses.

However, this book is not a mere academic essay in definition. Its main theme is that, whatever may have been the case in the past, liberalism is not suited to the conditions of the second half of the twentieth century and later—which we call "the postmodern world." The further America moves out of the modern and into the postmodern world, the more certain does it seem to us that the valid alternative to conservatism is no longer liberalism; it is communism.

The policies of President Johnson assume that there is no irreconcilable clash between liberals and conservatives. The President apparently believes it possible to hunt with the hounds and run with the hares on such issues as the budget, civil rights, anticommunism, government centralization, and all the rest.

The principle of the clear choice is that this is *not* possible. The intellectual dishonesty inherent in even the effort to do so is, on the other hand, the surest way to subvert democratic and republican government. It is the surest way to plunge this country into confusion and into darkness.

When all cats look gray—when sharp contrasts are no longer possible—then we will know the lights have gone out.

P. A. S.
S. B. M.

Acknowledgment

We are grateful for the patience and long-suffering forbearance of our wives, Kay Baden Sexson and Virginia Dyer Miles, during the writing and rewriting of this book—which entailed the painstaking preparation of eight or nine times as much material as now appears.

Our thanks go to other publishers to whom we submitted the manuscript who, though critical of certain points and reluctant to undertake publication on the expedited schedule we thought necessary, were almost uniformly complimentary of the book as a whole, and whose words of moral encouragement sustained us in many a weary hour. We particularly want to thank Edward Uhlan and his merrie men of Exposition Press for their yeomanly and cavalier, yet exquisitely deft, cutting of the manscript and their willingness to plunge into a headlong production schedule.

Without the unstinting interest, energy and time given by Mrs. L. W. "Rocky" Kuhn, who typed and retyped the manuscript, it would never have become a book. We feel that in a real sense this is her, as well as our, book.

P. A. S.
S. B. M.

Contents

doctrinally but also in the fact that liberalism is coming under the domination of politics, while conservatism retains its adherence to fixed principles. Moreover, and contrary to liberal propaganda, conservatism is necessarily a philosophy of moderation, while modern liberalism runs to extremes.

To the liberal, ideas are the important thing; to the conservative, people—whom he regards as spiritual and moral as well as physical and material beings—are. This basic conflict of values is reflected in the psychological make-up of liberals and conservatives.

Part Two THE MAJOR ISSUES

The liberal thinks of communism as an idea that will go away—or "mellow"—if treated gently; the conservative sees communism as destroying the character and souls of people.

The liberal, concentrating on ideas and theories to the exclusion of experience, traditions, attitudes, race, religions, background, nationality, and the other marks of individuality, sees no reason why all the world should not be under one "supra-government." The conservative warns that this ultra-centralization would destroy both individuality and sanity, as well as all the values the democratic and freedom-loving peoples hold dear.

The essence of the welfare state is its suppression of
any head-on collision, and its definition of "welfare"
in accordance with the preconceptions of those who
govern it. "Welfare" soon comes to mean "monolithic
powers."

For the conservative, "rights" become "wrongs" unless they are joined with "duties" and "responsibilities."
They cannot be so joined when government under-
writes them. Only by individuals proving their worth
by their own actions and acceptance of responsibility
can they really raise the level of the "rights" they are
entitled to.

Part Three   PERSPECTIVES

Liberalism, once adapted to its times, has outlived its
usefulness. It survives in the modern world not as a
force, but as a mystique that paralyzes action, decision,
character, energy, purpose. The objective of liberalism
today seems to be to make any forthright head-on collision impossible by obscuring all sharp points of difference and dissimilarity.

The conservative, now resurgent, is realizing how destructive the confused doctrines and paralysis of lib-

Introduction

The outstanding fact of American political life today is the resurgence of conservatism. The ascendancy of Barry Goldwater, the rising echelon of conservative spokesmen in Congress, the activity of young conservatives on the campus—these are the truly new and different developments on our political landscape, the visible signs of a great upheaval. Alongside them the latest variations in the faltering orthodoxy of liberalism are stale news Indeed, a fact which even the liberals themselves have come grudgingly to concede.

Nor is the conversative movement exclusively, or even primarily, political. It is rooted in a quest for value and certitude, for standards of right more permanent than yesterday's verdict at the ballot box. Conservative leaders, from Senator Goldwater to the college student debating with his roommate, are characteristically issue-oriented, concerned to measure public men and events in terms of principle. The rise of a conservative politics has thus been paralleled by the rise of a conservative intellectual community, manifest in the expanding circulation of *National Review,* the increasing demand for conservative books, the entry of conservative scholars into the once exclusive purviews of the liberal academy.

Although the conservative resurgence has been years in the making, its public career has been remarkably short. Because its

very existence is offensive to the reigning orthodoxy, the first
intimations of what was afoot, some ten and more years ago,
were smothered in disparagement or explained away or, most
effective of all, simply ignored. Liberalism had said so long there
could *be* no conservatism in America that many, including the
conservatives, believed it; so that when the movement at last became too restless and powerful to be wished away, it seemed to
burst upon the national consciousness out of nowhere. The resulting coalescence of varied centers of activity into a single
movement has therefore been abrupt and hectic and exhilarating.
In the past four years, the nation at large has come suddenly to
realize the conservatives are there. Even more decisively, perhaps, the conservatives themselves have come to realize they are
there, and have set to work to make their existence felt.

The outcome has been a tumultuous release of energy, a
somewhat haphazard articulation of conservative goals and prem-
ises, and not a little confusion: confusion generated by the ad-
versaries of conservatism, who have switched from tactful silence
to all-out blitzkrieg; confusion generated by enthusiasts whose
judgment is not equal to their intentions; confusion generated
by the very nature of the problem with which conservatives are
attempting to deal.

In the normal course of things, a deep shift in public sentiment may take a generation and more to achieve—beginning
with the unfolding of an idea to receptive minds, and emerging
in a few decades' time as the high policy of a nation. But the
American political drama can no longer proceed in such leisurely
fashion. The nation struggles for direction under the most griev-
ous danger in its history, a danger which hourly presses against
the frontiers of liberty, limiting the options and menacing the
security of the United States. The sands of time are running,
and there are few conservatives so sanguine as to believe that
there is a full generation remaining.

The conservative is therefore attempting, virtually overnight,
to do something which in a less desperate era might have taken
thirty years to accomplish: to achieve a reversal of national

momentum at the most fundamental level; to alter the politics of the nation, and to influence the thought processes by which that politics has come into existence. There are few men so fool-hardy as to think they have a certain formula for accomplishing so immense a task.

The authors of this book lay claim to no certain formula. They do lay claim to a broad-gauged understanding of the problem, and the nature of the difficulties which lie before American conservatism. Above all, they perceive the necessity of laying down priorities—of deciding which things should be done, how they should be done, and in what order. Should conservatives concern themselves principally with anti-Communism, or with diminishing the potencies of the domestic state, or with reforming the educational system? Or should they, seeking higher ground, emphasize the crisis at the source of all the others—the loss of faith and spiritual energy which has become so baleful a characteristic of our national life in all its departments?

Finally, there is a difference of opinion about technique as well as about substance. Is the problem political, or intellectual? Should conservatives invest their energies in an all-out battle for political supremacy, or cultivate an understanding worthy of a loftier success? Should they hurl themselves into the breach for Goldwater, or withdraw to the library to ponder the eloquence of Burke?

The dilemma which gives rise to these questions also dictates the answer, and it is not altogether satisfying. For the case seems to be that, to do any of these things properly, conservatives must be prepared to do all of them. Surely no temporal happiness can comfort us without the prop of spiritual vitality, while ethical regeneration in turn demands a regime of free choice as the context of decision. Political activity is needed to maintain working room and breathing space for the job of intellectual renewal, and political ambition without philosophy is simply the desire for power. To preserve American liberty the Cold War must be won, but the victory would be an empty one if that liberty should simultaneously decay from within.

In short, neither time nor the nature of the present crisis allows the subdivision of our distress into tidy categories, each to be handled in its turn. Liberalism is a total world view which begins with the notion of masterless man in the ethical realm, and arrives at the concept of regulated man in the political. It involves both religious presuppositions *and* the enginery of political dominion, and absorbs the whole range of issues from foreign policy to economics to civil rights which lie between. The errors of liberal ideology are shot through every zone of thought, interacting and sustaining one another so that cause and effect are difficult to isolate. Involving as it does radically opposed views of man, society, and the universe, the confrontation cuts across the whole range of human experience. And if conservatism is to succeed, if its success is to have content and meaning, it must engage liberalism on all fronts simultaneously.

The great virtue of the book Mr. Sexson and Mr. Miles have written is to perceive and expound this central truth with clarity and common sense. These are men whose immediate concerns are political, but who recognize that what happens in the political arena is in the last analysis dependent on what happens in the deeper realm of idea and principle. They recognize as well that no single department of the conservative-liberal struggle can be neglected in favor of another—that unless the challenge is handled decisively on a wide front, no single aspect of it is likely to be handled well.

The problem thus suggested is a difficult one: whether conservatism, simultaneously seeking intellectual regeneration and political realization, can rally the energies necessary for such a job. The answer depends upon the caliber of skill, dedication and understanding which the votaries of conservatism bring to the struggle. If the authors of this book are typical in their concern to unite practical policy with the deepest resources of principle, the outlook is bright indeed.

M. Stanton Evans

PART ONE

The Difference

CHAPTER ONE

The Head-on Collision

November 22, 1963, the date of the assassination of President John F. Kennedy, marked more than the death of a president. It symbolized the passing of the era of liberal supremacy. The country did not suddenly turn conservative on that date. Lyndon Johnson, who followed President Kennedy, sought earnestly to continue traditional liberal policies. But it was no use. Liberalism had started losing its self-confidence even before President Kennedy's murder. That President had been able to keep it going only by virtue of his personal charm and intellectual ability. Liberalism had already begun to resort more and more to illiberal means to keep itself in power: politicking, bossism, coercion, arm-twisting, Madison Avenue techniques, news management. Despite all this—or maybe because of it—it had become harder and harder to pull off any international or domestic successes, especially with the old liberal aplomb.

Before Mr. Kennedy's death there were many who blamed this lack of success on him. That, however, was neither right nor fair. Liberalism was failing first because its gossamer and dreamlike constitution was not suited to the rough world of the second half of the twentieth century, and second because, partly as a consequence, it was losing even the cohesive substance it once had.

Today we are living in a no man's land between conservatism, liberalism, and communism. As a living and a life-giving philosophy, conservatism, in the thinking of many, expired long ago —at the latest, by the middle 1930s. Liberalism is struggling desperately to restore fairyland, but it is finding increasingly that the world of the second half of the twentieth century is not made for either fairyland or liberalism itself. Communism, feared by nearly all and never able to generate any positive force, is greedily waiting until the destruction of morality and religion and purpose and human values has become complete. Let us look briefly at these three philosophies of the social order that are contesting not only for man's political allegiance, but for his soul. Let us start with conservatism, as the earliest.

Conservatism

During the 1930s conservatism was labeled "reaction." In the 1960s, "conservatism," to many, seems to mean "extremism." Neither, of course, is correct. The conservative knows better than anybody else that one can never really go back. He does not seek to retrieve the *conditions* of yesteryear; but he does believe, with Barry Goldwater, that "the laws of God, and of nature, have no dateline. The principles on which the conservative political position is based . . . are derived from the nature of man and from the truths that God has revealed about His creation . . . [which do not change]." And the conservative, intent on things as they are, rather than as some theory may tell him they should be, could never, never be an extremist.

Conservatism is not primarily a political concept, but a religious one. Probably the conservative's most fundamental belief is that "the Kingdom of God is within." He is against Big Government, not because he has any doubt about the surpassing need and utility of government in the modern age, but because government as we know it today seems to be seeking to become a rival of, or at least a surrogate for, God. The conservative is an individualist not in the sense of thinking that he is entitled to try to get whatever he as an individual wants, but because he believes that the underlying purpose of life is to enable each individual to prove himself. The conservative is inclined to accept the *status quo* as the place to start from, because he feels intuitively that there is a Divine design in the fact that things and people are as they are.

To the conservative there is no inner conflict between his recognition of utter dependence on God—whatever he may call Him—and his passion for freedom. The two are synonymous in practice. Freedom is what God gives man so he may prove himself.

There are, indeed, no inner conflicts in conservatism—period. To be sure, the conservative's world is made up of conflicts, but they are all conflicts of the outer world, or, to be more exact, between himself and the outer world. He sees things in terms of sharply contrasting opposites—of good and evil, black and white, night and day, man and woman, play and work, mine and not-mine, me and you, free and not-free. These opposites must both be allowed to clash and they must be held together. And held together they are: by the strength of his own character and personality, by recognition of the world as it is, by tradition, by convention, by compact, by authority, by duty and love, by man's physical and mental and moral needs—yes, even by prejudice.

In fact, the conservative is essentially one who "holds together" a world that has a built-in tendency to fall apart. This is the literal meaning of the word, derived from *cum*, meaning "with" or "together," and *servo*, meaning "keep," "hold," "guard." But for the conservative, the world is held together not in spite of head-on collisions, not by eliminating them, but because of the forces of opposition in the world, which together form a Divine harmony.

Liberalism

The liberal tradition is nearly as long as the conservative. In our civilization it goes back at least to the Renaissance, when the liberals of the time, known as "humanists," objected to the slow pace of society. The culture of the Middle Ages was too God-centered for the humanists; they felt that man in and of himself played a much larger role than was credited to him. The humanists, while carefully refraining from minimizing God, felt that science, secular education, art for art's sake should be more heavily stressed. They eventually became known as "liberals" because they called for freedom from the conventions, from traditions, and from authority.

The liberals called for freedom of scientific inquiry, freedom to say and write whatever they wanted to, freedom to attack and undermine old religious and social customs and patterns—freedom, in other words, to follow their own thinking wherever it led. Along with this demand for freedom went resentment against the members of society endowed with a more bountiful supply of the world's goods than the nascent liberals themselves had—which seemed manifestly unjust to them because they knew that, if anything, they themselves were more deserving. Besides, the liberals soon discovered that they were unable to obtain the kind of freedom they wanted as long as economic and political power remained concentrated in the hands of those they would henceforward mockingly, and sometimes more than a little enviously, refer to as "the conservatives."

Early in the history of liberalism therefore the demands for "liberty" and "equality" became inextricably intertwined. Almost at once, however, these two ingredients began pulling against each other, setting up inner tensions in the very texture of liberalism. The two facts that the liberals tried to blink away were (1) that equality, not being natural, could only be constrained, and (2) that the liberal brand of liberty, once reached, seemed in practice always to exacerbate the unequal condition of human beings. The dilemma of how to make "liberty" and "equality" compatible could readily be resolved by accepting the conservative definition of both concepts as limited by "what God hath wrought"—but it was the very essence of liberalism to revolt against the concept of God-centeredness.

The history of liberalism has been one long attempt to live with this inner contradiction. As long as the liberals were the opposition party, they were able to keep this problem under control. Even when they first gained power, it took time for the now rampaging liberals to snap the strands of social, economic, and political cohesion that the conservatives had woven together over centuries.

But the longer the liberals remained in power, the weaker became their bonds of cohesion, and the nearer liberalism itself came to being broken in two by the forces generated by its own inherent and basically antagonistic principles.

From this inner tension of liberalism came three developments. In the first place, liberalism proved basically unstable. While the fundamental conservative principles and definitions are the same today as they were yesterday, and will be the same tomorrow as today, the liberal doctrine has already passed through three diverse and more than a little contradictory phases: humanism, which emphasized the values of the individual mind; economic liberalism, which emphasized individual enterprise; and social liberalism, which emphasized individual welfare. It may now be passing into still another stage. As liberalism completed these phases, the parts of them that had stood the test of time were integrated into conservatism.

In the second place, liberalism, in constant danger of breaking up through internal contradictions, began to stress the virtue of glossing over conflicts and opposition. Originally the spice of life to the liberal, competition, and especially any possibility of a head-on collision, became increasingly feared and distrusted by him.

And in the third place, the liberal philosophy was constantly being readjusted and reanalyzed as conditions required a slightly different balance of freedom and equality. Liberal doctrines became more and more elaborate, and the liberals became recognizable by their distrust of simplicity and their yearning for the complicated.

Communism

While both liberalism and conservatism are philosophies of the individual, though in very different ways, communism is a philosophy of the mass. In communism, the individual is not important. The communist believes that individuals are only units of a collective, and that everything should be held "in common." This applies not only to property, but to wives and children, to ideas, to accomplishments. In its anti-individualism, communism is the obverse of both conservatism and liberalism.

If the difference between the latter two philosophies has to be oversimplified and put in a nutshell, it is this: to the conservative, the concept of God is more fundamental than the concept of freedom; to the liberal, freedom is more fundamental than God. The communist denies both God and freedom.

The conservative regards the communist philosophy as utterly repugnant and pure evil. He has no use at all for communism, and sees no merit in it. But the liberal and the communist have agreed to disagree. They are still on speaking terms. In a manner of speaking, the mission of the communist is to resolve the freedom/equality dilemma of the liberals by abolishing the concept of freedom. While the liberal can never accept the solution, he can appreciate it as a solution. The conservative cannot and will not go even that far.

Communism is not basically an economic or a political or even a social philosophy. It is far larger than its formulation by Karl Marx. Even Marx, however, was motivated more by his hatred for God than by his hatred for capitalism. All communists, like Marx in his time, are unwilling to believe in any authority greater than themselves—especially if, at the same time, they cannot even understand it. Atheism and unbridled egotism (an egotism, that is, without individuality) are, and have always been, the two main ingredients of communism. And unlike the case of liberalism, the two ingredients of communism are fully compatible with each other.

The communist does not even recognize government as his God. He gets around this by claiming that all-powerful government, though it may be necessary for a time under communism, is a transitory stage, and that eventually "the state will wither away." When that time comes, everything the government has held in trust for the people will, of course, pass on to the people themselves.

Like the conservative, and to some extent the liberal, the communist is well defined by his very name. The word "communism" can either be derived from *communis*, meaning "common," or from "commune," which refers the inquirer to the Commune of Paris established during the French Revolution. In either case the concept is definitely a citified, sophisticated one, stressing equality of economic and social status by outlawing all claims to distinction. The implications of "communism," however, are just the reverse of the term "community," so dear to the conservative, in which the accent was not on equality, but rather on the duty of each to live out the role God had cast him in; and of "common sense" and "common law," which recognize that right thinking is more than intellectual brilliance, and that law is more than the codification of legal formulas.

The whole edifice of communism takes on the shape of one long negation; no God, no private property (which has the same implication as just "no property" would), no individual responsibility, no individual initiative, no absolute morality, no objective right and wrong, no life transcending death, no unselfishness, no enduring Purpose.

Liberalism vs. Communism

These three—call them "ideologies" if you must—compete for a world that, as the year 1963 ended, seemed to be a no man's land because it was so obviously out of control, at least by man. Each of these three "ideologies" is fighting, or at least resisting, the other two. What does this mutual resistance look like?

First, let us consider liberalism versus communism. On the liberal side this conflict is characterized by a feeling that communism can be made to mellow, and that communists, for all practical purposes, would then become liberals—if they are not really so already. (The communist, on the other hand, sees himself as the heir of the liberal and is waiting only for liberalism, a concept that he tends to identify with "capitalism," to fall of its inner contradictions.)

"The crime of the USSR against the world is its determination to make experimentation in libertarian socialism impossible," wrote Arthur M. Schlesinger, Jr., professional liberal and presidential assistant under Kennedy, in 1947, in the *Partisan Review*. This is still the prevailing attitude of the liberals who are likely to regard communism as a liberal heresy. They tend to overlook the faithlessness of the communist regime, its butchery and double-dealing and brazenness and bigotry and pettiness of spirit and meanness and implacability, and concentrate on the failure of the communists, at the time of the Revolution and since, to use the rout of the conservatives to establish a liberal utopia.

But the liberals do not believe that all is yet lost in Russia and the other communist countries. By sweet reasonableness and other liberal techniques, the liberals hope to persuade the communists to reform. They shudder at the idea of a head-on collision with the communists, which to them means war, rather than the way to avoid war, and insist that communism can be melted by kindness. The liberal doctrine simply does not recognize evil.

Wherever the liberal looks he sees only grays, never blacks and whites.

The communist, for his part, is quite willing to accept the liberal's kindnesses and clumsy attempts at conciliation—especially because he knows they exacerbate the internal strains within liberalism. But the communist, as long as he remains a communist, simply cannot respond with kindness and genuine friendship. The conservative would say this was because communism *is* pure evil. In any event, fear, suspicion, and distrust are too deeply ingrained in the communist for him voluntarily to cooperate with anyone, even a fellow communist, except either through coercion or through communist indoctrination.

While the liberal is wedded to the soft approach, the communist is even more convinced that his only chance is to be tough.

Liberalism vs. Conservatism

When liberalism and conservatism, rather than liberalism and communism, are opposed, the conflict is a very different one. But there is one outstanding similarity: the conservative (as does the communist) seeks the head-on collision; the liberal, in both cases, tries to avoid it. The liberal, let us say again, simply sees no point in it. Just as, for the liberal, the communist is a heretical liberal, so the conservative is an undeveloped liberal, one who has not yet been enlightened. In both cases the liberal believes that to draw hard-and-fast lines and then plunge in to the attack would be just the wrong thing to do. Rather than a contest of guts, bluff, and endurance against the communist, or of sharp political debate with no holds barred and no favors asked against the conservative, the liberal feels the answer is more education—for the communist and the conservative, of course.

Years ago, the liberals were more willing to trade punch for punch with the conservatives and allow the voters to decide the winner; they are not so now. In the thirties, for instance, the fact that the United States was a democracy seemed to operate to the benefit of the liberals, and they were therefore more willing to "let the people judge." But no more. There is hardly any liberal today who does not sense the fact that the people are deserting him—and "going conservative" with a rush. Actually, most people have always been conservative. The only change is that more of them now realize it.

During the thirties and forties, "conservative" was a term of derision. The testimony of a witness during a court trial of a man accused of disturbing the peace is typical of the prevailing attitude. The witness, testifying against the defendant, said, "He was using abusive language, calling people conservative and all that."

Almost everyone wanted to be considered a "liberal." That word sounded glamorous—and undeniably liberals had done great things in the past. Then, a small but growing band of statesmen in Washington announced themselves as conservatives, and began to show by their words, their actions, and their personalities what conservatism was. Partly as a result of this, and partly because the times were becoming ripe for conservatism again, people by the millions began recognizing themselves as conservatives.

In December, 1962, a Gallup poll found that the percentage of the population preferring conservatism had already caught up to that preferring liberalism: 28 per cent to 27 per cent, with 45 per cent declining to state a preference or describing themselves as middle-of-the-roaders. In July, 1963, seven months later, a Harris poll found 34 per cent of the voters classifying themselves as conservatives, with liberals representing only 24 per cent and the rest 42 per cent. If the two polls were comparable, the conservatives, during the first half of 1963, were increasing at the rate of about a million a month, while the number of liberals was decreasing almost a half million a month.

This great conversion, reflected in the swell in Goldwater

support in 1962 and 1963, was temporarily halted by the death of President Kennedy and the momentary success of the liberal effort to tag the conservatives as "extremists." But it was again on the upswing at the time this book went to press.

In addition to their doctrinal dislike of the HOC (head-on collision), therefore, liberals in the United States have another very good reason for trying to gloss over or duck any sharp divergences on issues: this is coming, everything else being equal, to be their only way of winning national elections. Contrariwise, it is to the interest of the conservatives to insist on debates, arguments, discussion—everything, in fact, that could sharpen the issues and illuminate the liberal-conservative contrast.

Conservatism vs. Communism

Liberalism today is chiefly important as an obstacle. As such it does very well indeed in some ways. But it is outside the mainstream of events. The two great movements of our time are conservatism and communism. The ultimate head-on collision will be between these two.

Let us hasten to say that by this we do not mean to predict an eventual *military* war between the forces of conservatism and those of communism. For the conservative at least the showdown would take the form of economic, diplomatic, and psychological warfare backed by overwhelming armaments, by a maximum of individual initiative, individual responsibility, and individual imagination, and by a state of moral preparedness for any eventuality.

The victor in this head-on collision would probably be decided in the end by the comparative strength of the two secret weapons. The communist's secret weapon is his willingness to lie. This is no doubt what Nikita Khrushchev meant by saying that "my secret weapon is my tongue." The willingness to say anything, the splitting of words from their meaning, double-talk and double-think, utter faithlessness on the part of a great nation, is indeed a fearsome weapon.

The secret weapon of the conservatives is their belief that the most important things are not of this world. Conservatives are willing to face death, if necessary, in the serene assurance that it is not the end. But for communists, and for many, if not most, liberals, the loss of their earthly life is indeed the end. There is no Beyond. Therefore, if the communist is threatened with war (the threat of war would be part of the head-on collision between communism and conservatism, even though war itself would probably not be) in a way that is thoroughly convincing to him, he would back down and wait until a more opportune time, as he has always done to date.

The Head-on Collision

Both conservatism and communism believe in the direct approach. The liberal likes to do things by indirection. This liberal indirection—it borders on intellectual dishonesty—is the greatest threat to freedom, other than communism itself, in the world today.

Kind treatment of Russia is supposed to soften up communism. It doesn't. During the era of fairyland softness, still persisting, communism has expanded to cover half the world.

The Western cause is supposed to have benefited from official and unofficial American intervention in China, Korea, Cuba, Laos, Katanga, and South Vietnam, which had the effect of discouraging vigorous (perhaps overvigorous) pro-Western and anticommunist policies and supporting or appearing to support more "neutral" or even pro-communist elements. It didn't.

United States foreign aid, even when it wound up in hostile or potentially hostile countries, was supposed to be in the best interests of the American people because it would help to create a "middle class." It didn't—and it wasn't.

Government subsidization of American farmers, to get them to raise fewer crops, is supposed to be the way to increase farm income and solve the farm problem. Instead, it has made that problem greater than ever, and the farmers are sick of the government program.

Deficit spending is supposed to be the way to balance the budget, and more tax revenue is supposed to be produced by tax cuts. So far, deficit spending has only added to debt and inflation.

Right-to-work laws are supposed to threaten economic freedom. Professors and whiz kids are supposed to know more about military strategy and tactics than generals and admirals. National security is supposed to be enhanced by getting rid of zealous anticommunists in government. Religion is supposed to benefit from outlawing prayers and Bible reading in schools. In a hundred other ways liberals seem to hope to accomplish an objective by adopting policies that a man of common sense would have said, a few years ago, were nicely calculated to circumvent that objective.

Perhaps the liberals do know what they are doing. In a dictatorship, which many of them seem to be developing a liking for, perhaps they would be suffered to continue until they *do* prove their point—if they have one.

But in a democracy the people, most of whom are not terribly sophisticated, and practically all of whom believe in direct action, will tolerate this apparent denial of common sense only as long as it seems to be producing satisfactory results.

Domestically and especially internationally, the results of the apparent rejection of common sense by liberals are not satisfactory today—and they show promise of being even less satisfactory tomorrow.

The American people want at least to *try* to meet their problems. The liberals seem to be grappling with little else but straw men. Most people do not really know whether the liberal or the conservative solution is better, but they have a persistent feeling of disquiet, as though something is wrong that they cannot lay their finger on—and they long for a head-on collision between liberalism and conservatism that might help them decide where to put that finger. Finally, they long for leaders with the guts to accept head-on collisions.

CHAPTER TWO

Liberalism Divides; Conservatism Unites

Liberalism is an interloper on the American political scene. Although some of our statesmen, from earliest times, have been deeply influenced by liberal thought from Europe, and although some of the origins of the lunatic left can be traced back to Reconstruction days and even further, both of the major political parties were founded as conservative, and remained conservative down to 1912. The conservatism of the Jeffersonian Democrats reflected the distrust of Thomas Jefferson, the aristocrat, for any centralization of power, financial or governmental, and his preference for local and states' rights over federalism. The conservatism of the Lincoln Republicans reflected the profound devotion of Abraham Lincoln, man of the people, to law, especially constitutional law. For both Jefferson and Lincoln, it goes without saying, people, traditions, and our free institutions and national sovereignty were more important than abstract ideas.

Given this send-off, the precise nature of the conservatism of the two parties grew, not out of doctrines or learned treatises, but out of the interests and habits of thought that each represented. The Democrats were mainly Southerners and Westerners, and accordingly their party came to stand for low tariffs, free silver (which meant, for practical purposes, a moderate degree of inflation), trust busting (especially of railroads, on which Westerners were so dependent), and more direct democracy.

All four policies were in line with their economic interests, which required bigger export markets and higher prices for their agricultural produce, low prices for the merchandise they bought, relief from the burden of indebtedness, protection from gorging by the railroads, and possession of a whip hand over governmental bodies suspected of being dominated by eastern industrial and financial interests.

On the other hand, after Grant, the Republicans were mainly Easterners. Their greatest practical concern was to secure and expand markets for the output of their infant industries, and after that to insure stable property rights. For the first objective they needed protective tariffs to keep out lower-priced foreign goods, as well as a sound money system to ward off inflation, which would defeat the purpose of the tariff by raising the manufacturer's own costs and prices higher than the tariffs raised foreign prices. For the second objective they also sought sound money, which would prevent inflationary confiscation of a part of their investments. They sought, in addition, a strong government able to defend property rights and maintain a wholesome industrial climate.

Russell Kirk somewhere points out, following Edmund Burke, that politics must be based either on interests or on ego. To base politics on interests was, until about fifty years ago, the American way. It was also the conservative way.

The Democratic Party Is Uprooted

Sectional interests dominated both parties until well into the twentieth century. Around the turn of the century, two events took place that shook the Democrats loose. One of these events was the organization of the Intercollegiate Society of Socialists in 1905. The I.S.S., as Stanton Evans records, began as a purely campus venture, with the purpose of awakening "an interest in socialism among the educated men and women of the country." In this, he notes, it succeeded beyond all expectations. Alumni of the I.S.S. include "labor leaders David Dubinsky, Al Hayes, Andrew Biemiller, Jay Lovestone, Walter and Victor Reuther; academicians Leonard Doob, Talcott Parsons, Harold Faulkner, and Sidney Hook; journalists Murray Kempton, Max Lerner, James Wechsler, and Joe Lash (all of the New York *Post*), Freda Kirchwey, Bruce Bliven, Walter Lippmann, and government servants Ralph Bunche and Paul Porter." On their shoulders has fallen much of the burden of supporting liberalism for the last thirty years.

The second event, or rather series of events, brought these I.S.S. graduates their opportunity. A decade or so before the formation of the I.S.S., the Democratic Party began breaking away from its traditional West and South moorings. In his second administration Democratic President Grover Cleveland forced the repeal of the Sherman Silver Purchase Act, throwing his party into confusion. This confusion was compounded when, after vainly nominating William Jennings Bryan, a progressive (but certainly not a liberal) Westerner, in 1896 and 1900, his party selected the gold Democrat, Alton B. Parker, as standard bearer in 1904. This proving a failure also, Bryan sought to unite the western, southern, and eastern wings of the party behind his candidacy, for a third time, in 1908, but succeeded only in alienating many of his western supporters, who accused him of selling out to the big city bosses, and who then went over to the progressive Republicanism of Theodore Roosevelt. After 1908, the interest base of the Democratic Party was in ruins. In 1912, profiting from the split between the Taft Republicans and the Roosevelt Bull Moosers, the Democrats finally captured the White House. But the successful candidate represented neither the agrarian West and South nor the industrial East. That successful candidate was our first liberal president, Woodrow Wilson, who found advisers from among the I.S.S. alumni.

The Democratic Party Becomes the Liberal Party

Wilson, with his dreams, his theories, his conviction that the end (a vague internationalism) justifies the means, and his inability to deal with determined men, had little appeal to the farmers and small-town people of the West. That section of the country loyally helped to re-elect him in 1916, but through its senators it broke him in 1919—and then deserted the Democratic Party, which has never been the same since. The collapse that began under Cleveland now seemed fatal.

From 9.1 million in 1916, the Democratic presidential vote sank, despite the woman's suffrage amendment and the growth of population, to 8.3 million in 1924. The party seemed on the way out. Then came the alliance between the I.S.S. men, some of whom had been given a taste of political power under Wilson, and the bosses of the big-city political machines. The first step in the re-creation of the Democratic Party was the nomination, in 1928, of Alfred E. Smith, New Yorker, which gathered in the Catholic vote and greatly increased its pulling power in the East. In 1932, aided by the depression, the Alliance (now known as political liberalism) catapulted Franklin D. Roosevelt into the White House. Almost immediately the groundwork began for the famous "coalition of minorities," which has dominated American politics ever since.

Liberal Collection of Minorities

The six minorities, with collectively well over two-thirds of the nation's vote, which Smith-Roosevelt-Truman-Stevenson-Kennedy nailed together, comprised (1) those without a high-school education, (2)members of labor unions and their families, (3) Catholics, (4) southerners, (5) Negroes, and (6) Jews. This coalition became emphatically a liberal, rather than a Democratic, one. The single common denominator of the six was that they *did* feel themselves to be aggrieved minorities—perhaps the surest characteristic of liberalism. The poorly educated found it hard to get along in today's world. Labor unionists have always imagined themselves as "the downtrodden." The Catholics were only just emerging from a period when their religion was an economic and social handicap. Southerners remembered the War between the States. The Negroes were resentful of past slavery and present discrimination. And the Jews were always on the lookout for anti-Semitism. Liberalism in its practical aspects is a past master at exploiting all these resentments and humiliations and hatreds. Moreover, it created the illusion of "doing something" for each. Even better, most of these groups were sufficiently docile for the big-city bosses, labor bosses, segregationist leaders, and racial organizations to be able to hold them in line.

Those without much education seemed to benefit from liberal legislation guaranteeing the social security they felt ill equipped to earn on their own. Labor got recognition of its unions, better contracts, maximum hours, and minimum wages. The Catholics were enabled twice to vote for a Catholic for president, and once to elect him. The one-party system in the South enabled the Southerners to keep segregation. Every four years, Negroes got promises of an expansion of civil rights. Jews were tied to the liberal coalition by the Rooseveltian anti-Nazi policy during the thirties.

Political Erosion of Liberalism

The year 1936 was the high point for liberalism in the United States. In that year Roosevelt amassed 35 per cent of the vote of the total electorate. During the next twenty years liberal support almost continuously receded, as is shown in Table I. In spite of the great growth in population, the Democratic vote was not again to attain the numerical size of Roosevelt's second election, and in percentage Democratic support sank to 25 per cent of the potential.

In 1960, as they did in 1928, the Democrats nominated a Catholic to pep up a failing party. The strategy seemed to work. Table II shows that the Catholic votes, which had receded from the Democratic Party when Adlai Stevenson was the nominee, flowed back to support John F. Kennedy—about 81 per cent, according to the Michigan Survey Research Center.

In 1960, liberalism undeniably took a political spurt, but probably for the last time. By 1964, the fundamental weakness of the "strategy of minorities" had been exposed. Most of the six groups were fighting among themselves, or showing signs of wanting to do so. And all of them were channeling their dissatisfaction, not so much against the conservative *status quo,* which liberalism has traditionally hoped to change, but against the new (and unstable) *status quo* of the Johnson regime.

Civil rights agitation, accompanied by the forced integration of southern universities and favoritism to Negroes in governmental and government-related jobs, made it very clear that the interests of the Negro minority were in head-on collision not only with the interests of the southern white minority, but with certain northern white minorities too.

Later chapters will explore in some detail the dawning realization on the part of each of the six minorities (including the Negro) that, in an age of preoccupation with international problems, peace and defense, racial disputes, and automation, liberalism just did not have its old appeal. At the same time, the old frictions within liberalism were being exacerbated and new ones added.

The liberal is the traditional foe of the Catholic; this is recognized in continental Europe, and it is only a question of time before the American Catholic too realizes his natural allegiance is to conservatism. Labor has found the liberal good at helping to get wages increased and unions recognized, but is bound to begin realizing that, with the most pressing problem facing it today

TABLE I

DEMOCRATIC VOTE FOR PRESIDENT

Year	Democratic Vote (millions)	Potential Electorate (millions)	Democratic Vote as Percentage of Electorate
1920	9.1	61.0	15
1924	8.4	65.6	13
1928	15.0	70.4	21
1932	22.8	75.0	30
1936	27.8	79.4	35
1940	27.2	83.5	33
1944	25.6	85.2	30
1948	24.1	94.5	27
1952	27.3	98.9	28
1956	24.0	103.2	25
1960	34.2	107.9	32

TABLE II

ESTIMATED DIVISION OF VOTE IN PRESIDENTIAL ELECTIONS OF 1956 AND 1960, BY RELIGIOUS AFFILIATION OF VOTER

Candidate	Est. No. of Catholic Votes	Est. No. of Other Votes	Total
Eisenhower (1956)	8 million	28 million	36 million
Stevenson (1956)	7 million	19 million	26 million
Kennedy (1960)	14 million	20 million	34 million
Nixon	3 million	31 million	34 million

being the preservation of jobs in an era of increasing automation, the liberal is not equipped to give any real help other than perhaps a dole for those who become "unemployable." (The conservative, on the other hand, is, by definition, interested in slowing down change of all types and making it more assimilable.) The less well educated will realize that the liberal intellectuals are already writing him off as "obsolescent," and that the ballyhooed Johnson program of ending poverty is restricted for the most part to those who are still in school, or at least still young. The less well-educated minority will have to look increasingly toward the conservative, who proverbially places more emphasis on experience and less on formal education. Southerners, struggling to preserve their traditions, are realizing that liberals do not care a fig for traditions. The Negro, over whom liberals weep copious tears, is finding that they promise big but perform little—while conservatives can be relied on for gradual, if unglamorous, improvement. And the Jews, possibly the most enterprising group of all, will not continue forever to back the anti-Nazi party of the thirties when its interference in their personal fortunes and personal plans becomes intolerable.

As the underlying conditions of the sixties (the cold war, communism, automation, racial conflict, foreign understandings and alliances) replace the underlying conditions of the thirties (depression, unemployment, fascism, social reform), the whole idea of the New Deal–Fair Deal–New Frontier begins to seem obsolete. On his accession to power, President Johnson inherited the good will of the American people to a surprising degree, partly out of hope that he would become a "new Roosevelt." But it was too late. The magic of liberalism could no longer cement together the quarreling groups into which a liberal America had become divided.

The Thirties and the Sixties

The 1930's were an ideal time for the liberals to come to power. While both domestic and international affairs were awry, the domestic problem seemed much the more pressing. To enshrine Franklin Roosevelt and his followers in the hearts of millions required only promises and brave words, accompanied by an expansion of government and a few reforms. In 1932, the United States was in the pit of a depression, with signs of buoyancy already having appeared on several occasions. When Roosevelt took over we were at the bottom, and not even ill-advised New Deal measures could deepen that bottom. When things got better, the New Dealers were given credit for everything that happened. (Which was not too breath-taking. American Federation of Labor figures show that after eight years of prodigious Rooseveltian efforts, unemployment at the beginning of 1940 was still 10,650,000—not quite one million less than the 11,586,000 at the time of Roosevelt's election.)

Even if Roosevelt is credited with restoring prosperity and ending depression unemployment, which few of even the more rabidly liberal economists claim, it would be almost irrelevant in the climate of the sixties. Almost everything "went" in the early Roosevelt years; the people approved almost every type of "action." And the action of the Roosevelt administration was of the sledge-hammer type; with very little of the finesse required in the present delicately balanced world situation. Topheavy Democratic (and docile) majorities in Congress; an atmosphere often approaching panic; propaganda, political skill, dedication—these were the ingredients of the Rooseveltian magic. Even during the war years, when operations were on an unprecedently vast scale, the Roosevelt manipulations, compared with the ones needed today, were essentially simple. An error in the thirties could be covered up by another appropriation; an error in the sixties (one that cost us, say, the loyalty of an ally) could doom the world.

Ideals and Imperialism

While liberalism flourishes when turned loose on domestic problems, it has always been helpless when confronted with international ones, especially when war was not in question. The liberal may be good with the sledge hammer, but he has no ability with the rapier. Domestically, the liberal could pose as a man of constructive ideas; the emergence of the world stage has made it clear that his forte is really destruction.

Consider the liberal's passion against "imperialism." Primarily because of insistent pressure by American liberals, England, France, the Netherlands, and Belgium found it impossible to keep their colonies and "dominions." The outcome has been to spread disorder and communism in Asia, and riot, massacre, rape, and torture in Africa. Chaos, savagery, and fascism have been the result of the attempt, on a world scale, to apply liberal ideals, which shuddered to see one nation with less liberty or equality than another.

Historically, liberalism has been noted for these ideals. During the 1930s and before, liberal ideals, then in full flower, were indeed a powerful unifying force. They proved particularly attractive in America, where they operated most effectively to temper the prevailing conservatism. But in a nonconservative world liberal ideals simply corrupt; they even corrupt the liberals themselves.

Even at best, liberalism was rarely, if ever, able (or willing) to trace the practical consequences of its ideals. Seldom did they prove out in a way that all could see. But while liberals were excluded from power, to use that argument against them was only academic. And even after liberalism finally came to power, the liberal could attribute any failure to realize his ideals to a conspiracy by anti-idealistic "interests" (that is, conservatives). He could remain invincibly convinced of his own rightness and the conservative's wrongness.

In drawing a distinction between liberal and conservative, J. Kenneth Galbraith, for instance, contemptuously dismisses the conservative as "led by a disposition, not unmixed with pecuniary self-interest, to adhere to the familiar and the established." "But the liberal," says Galbraith, "brings moral fervor and passion, even a sense of righteousness" to his ideas.

The De-idealization of Liberalism

In the nineteen twenties and thirties, the liberals constantly denounced conservatives as "materialistic," "crass," "greedy," "stodgy," "unimaginative," "vulgar," "stagnant," "regimented." But by the sixties it was the liberals who were the prime materialists. The conservatives were seeking—as shown in the writings of such men as Senator Goldwater and Russell Kirk, and in conversation with ordinary conservative businessmen, farmers, taxicab drivers, postmen, housewives, great-grandmothers, army officers, and so on—to recover some measure of moral and spiritual values.

On the other hand, while liberals still denounced conservatives for supporting such things as advertising, the profit system, and the free market, what did the liberals want to replace them with? Let Arthur M. Schlesinger, Jr., tell us.

In his *Politics of Hope* the man who, under Kennedy, became America's crown liberal, repeatedly takes potshots at the materialistic values resulting from private enterprise. "While we overstuff ourselves as individuals," he says, "we let the national plant run down." "We are heading," he says, "for the classical condition of private opulence and public squalor." What does Professor Schlesinger want? Why, he wants us to spend our money, not in the "private sector" but on enlarging "community services and facilities—schools, medical care, roads, recreation, water resources, and energy development." These are somehow better, he seeks to assure us, than the products of private enterprise—food, housing, clothing, newspapers, automobiles, television, private medicine.

Not a word does Schlesinger say about spiritual and religious values, character building, heroism and self-sacrifice, chivalry, courtesy, love, honor. The best the liberal can do is simply to substitute the God-word "public" for the devil-word "private."

The liberals, with their pious mien, have become the true materialists. Regimentation and vulgarity lurk in the prying into the private lives inseparable from the administration of the liberal's welfare state. Liberals are greedy to keep on making more and more "social gains," even at the expense of national strength. Almost everything about social security, unemployment compensation, payments to farmers, relief, and so on, is becoming more and more stodgy, unimaginative and stagnant. Brawls thrown by bureaucrats hit the jackpot for pure crassness; the high point of cynicism in this century may well have been the 1960 dumping of Nixon ballots into the Chicago River. For pure materialism, few conservatives can match Harry Hopkins's remark about "spending and spending, taxing and taxing, electing and electing," or the alliance between high-minded Washington intellectuals and the corrupt big-city bosses. And when, as in the case of Bertrand Russell and at least some of the authors of *The Liberal Papers*, liberals admit they would rather be red than dead, it becomes apparent that liberal ideals *are* already dead.

No wonder the late C. Wright Mills, himself a liberal, asked whether liberal ideals "must be given up or drastically revised, or whether there are ways of rearticulating them that retain their old moral force in a world that liberals never made." No wonder that Clarence Streit, also a liberal, finds a cleavage, a schizophrenia, within liberalism "that makes our world seem so mad."

When, in its palmy days, liberalism indignantly rejected self-interest as the base in politics and economics, it substituted its ideals. With the cracking of these ideals—or, to say the same thing in different words, their exposure as nothing but a jaded version of conservative self-interest translated from the "private sector" to the "public sector"—no central tendency at all is left to hold liberal political support together. The result, in politics, is that the liberal "strategy of minorities" is coming apart at the seams.

Liberal Out of His Element

But what has caused the tragic decline of liberal ideals? The liberal accession to power. The liberal is curiously unsuited to authority of any kind. Historically, his role has been to stand outside the government and criticize or offer suggestions. The liberal is the man of theory, of knowledge, of intellect—and as such has a very useful function. His job is to write books and articles, make speeches, engage in debate, issue pamphlets, organize effective opposition, lead crusades for better government, agitate for reforms, and the like. He often does a brilliant job in these matters. But as an executive in government, or in business for that matter, the liberal usually turns in a very mediocre performance. He is not a good supervisor or a good decision maker. He doesn't understand people, nor is he really interested in them —at least not when they come at him one by one, although liberals do seem to be terrifically interested in "people" as an abstraction. Nor, as long as he remains a true liberal, does he even *like* to exercise authority, let alone understand it or do it well.

Liberals have never grown accustomed to the uses of power. Talk to one. Even if he is a man whose slightest word may change the fate of nations, you will find he is preoccupied with criticism and self-justification. He likes to foregather with other liberals and discuss away the ills of the world, but he seldom knows what to *do* about them—except, perhaps, pass a bill. Indeed, to take any real action may never occur to him. The liberal thinks as an underdog. Today, though, he has to pretend to be top dog. The pretense is wearing thin. One of the first casualties has been the traditional liberal ideal, which could not stand up under a constant life of pretense, inexpert wielding of power, and repeated failures. The liberal in power seems to be able to take effective action only by chipping away a little more at his ideals.

The Liberal Lapse From Reality

But again we must ask ourselves: Why is the liberal so well cast as the loyal opposition and so miscast in government? Why can the liberal in power act only at the cost of his traditional ideals? The answer is that the liberal, as a liberal, thinks so much in terms of *should* that he simply fails to see the *is*. The liberal, as a liberal, is unable to handle realities. So the liberal, as a power man, has to split his personality.

In dealing with words and abstractions, the liberal often does surprisingly well. But the greatest problems of government, especially today, are the problems of dealing with people—how to handle Khrushchev, De Gaulle, Castro, Mao, Tshombe or other Tshombes, U Thant, Franco, Negroes, labor leaders, congressmen and senators, industrialists, anticommunists, rival politicians—men one doesn't like but whose good will he needs? The theories of liberalism help very little here.

Neither do they help much even with the impersonal problems of the sixties—which are problems of a different world away from the ones the liberal learned about in school. Should defense money be spent on manned bombers or missiles—and if missiles, what kind of missiles? At what point in a multi-billion-dollar defense project can we determine whether it will be a success or a failure? What expenditure on defense is "enough"? How much is "enough" on welfare? At what point does deficit spending cease to be a "blessing" and become a hazard? Just how should news be managed so that government derives the maximum benefit at the least risk of slipping up somewhere? How can Negroes be given just enough to keep them happy but not enough to antagonize too many white Democrats? Just how much independence can we allow our allies to exercise? Should we crack down on businessmen before or after they have a chance to attend a $1,000-a-plate party dinner? How much corruption is winning an election

worth? When does the legal operation of paying election workers become the illegal operation of buying votes?

And on the biggest question of all, what are the intentions
of communism? The liberal's insistence on giving the most benevolent answer to this question that he can get away with has
played a major part in bringing the age of Kennedy to an end.
The liberal just does not believe the repeated warnings of Lenin,
Stalin, and Khrushchev that "we will bury you." The liberal
doesn't understand the requirements of power freed from moral
and religious restraints as it necessarily exists under communism.
He doesn't credit the abject slavery of the communist-dominated
mind, nor the inhuman conditions behind the Iron Curtain. As a
result, the liberal indefatigably seeks "accommodation" with the
Soviet, pares our defenses, sacrifices our nuclear strength for the
advantages of having an "agreement" with the communists, can-
cels the very weapons that could prove decisive in a showdown,
and blithely spends billions on a flight to the moon while neglect-
ing the very areas of inner space where a commanding Soviet
lead would put us at the mercy of the communists.

To answer problems in the liberal way, it is necessary first to
apply liberal ideals—in a world, as C. Wright Mills so eloquently
admits, "liberals never made." As a result we get confused welfare programs, confused farm programs, confused foreign aid,
confusion in our policies toward almost all foreign nations from
Russia and China to South Vietnam and Cyprus, confusion between tax cuts and punitive expeditions against the "rich,"
confused civil rights attitudes, confusion, confusion, confusion.
The conservative, who believes the starting point is not ideals but
the world as it is, would have been able to avoid this confusion
and divisiveness.

When George Washington and his aides, after Yorktown, were
discussing, with some foreboding, the possibility that Congress
might hang Lord Cornwallis, one of them is reported to have re-
marked that it was not those who knew the world but those who
didn't who were the dangerous ones. In the same way, the lib-

erals, let loose in the arena of power, are dangerous. The liberal *has* learned to think, at least with words, but he is finding that thinking isn't enough. For one thing, the liberal today finds himself in the strange place of not knowing for what purpose he thinks. Because he doesn't see what is in front of him, and has lost his common sense, he is confused about final ends, values, goals. The best he can do is to assume that the ultimate aim is power itself. But the power man believes in coercion, not in the free exercise of intelligence nor in any other principle of liberalism. And the power man cares little for the liberal ideal of improving social and economic conditions—except his own. The liberal, floating in the empty space of unreality but pushed inexorably by the need to exercise power, can go nowhere except toward destruction.

The Illusion and the World

Again let us say that in this book we are not criticizing liberalism itself, but only liberalism when allied with power, and only the liberalism of the dawning postmodern era. As a minority sentiment, liberalism is often admirable. We, the authors of this book, do not happen to be liberals and we do not believe many of our readers (or, for that matter, our nonreaders) are. But, even so, there are many fine things to be said about the liberals.

When they get into power, however, liberals seem bent on dissolving the connective tissues of society. They almost confess this. Liberal Daniel Bell, for instance, has admitted that "the historic contribution of liberalism was to separate law from morality." Liberalism has gone far toward also separating politics and economics and philosophy and education and information from morality. And morality, more than any other force, is what holds society together.

Divisiveness, then, is inseparable from liberalism in power. How about conservatism in power?

The basic principle of conservatism is that a man must be himself. And he learns to be himself, not by dreaming dreams, thinking up ideas, or reading books, but by constantly rubbing against the whetstone of life. All those who do this seem to end up with remarkably similar convictions.

They learn, for instance, that they cannot have their cake and eat it too. They learn that they must be thankful for what they are and for what has been given them, as Burke said, by a "Divine tactic"—and that if they do not use it and enjoy it, it will be taken away. They learn that a man cannot be a real man unless he is proud of his God, his country, his family, his friends, and himself. They learn that a man must feel responsible for himself and his dependents, or he does not feel himself a man. They learn that human nature is the one constant in a world of continual change. They learn that their own gross appetites and passions, and those of other men, must be perpetually restrained by self-discipline, checks and balances, competition, quest for profits. They learn that, if instead of restraining these appetites and passions, we destroy them, we also destroy the source from which an individual gets his strength. They learn that enduring cooperation can only be based on the self-interest of each of the cooperating parties, and that any other apparent base is sheer illusion, which eventually takes the wavering shape of plain ego. They learn that all mortals seek integrity, and that if we commit a crime or break a moral law it is because our basic character has become so bent out of shape that the only possible integrity is a crooked one. They learn that no man can approach perfection, and that it is folly to hope for a permanent solution to man's problems, since he is put here precisely that he may be tested by problems.

All this and much more the conservative learns, usually without realizing that he is learning it, and almost always without seeking to put it into words. While the liberal is thinking up abstract ideas and reading books, the conservative is finding out what the world *is*.

And because all can appreciate the *is* and cooperate on the basis of it, conservatism can and does unite rich and poor, labor and business, city man and farmer, Jew and Gentile, Protestant and Catholic, Negro and white, the old Democratic West and South with the old Republican East.

Building on the Isn't

And the liberals? They willingly pass up this chance for unity. Half of them seem to believe that the highest employment of *status quo*, even after a generation or two of dominant liberalism, is to use it as something to get away from. All of them seem to believe that their most potent weapon against conservatism is to accuse the conservative of being content with the *status quo*, or of being the party of memory rather than hope, or of revering tradition.

No conservative wants to, or believes he can, stop change. Change is an inherent feature of the Divine Plan. But change of the intensity of the last fifty years threatens man's social and individual identity. And identity, the conservative knows, is the one thing he must fight to preserve. When it is not necessary to change, the conservative knows, it is necessary not to change.

But what has the liberal been doing? Why, as soon as he gets in a position of power, he starts trying to change things for the sake of change itself. It was not necessary for us to enter World War I. It was not necessary for us to set up a centralized Federal Reserve banking system. It was not necessary for us to set off on a governmentally encouraged inflationary spree during the twenties. It was not necessary for us to shift power from the states to the federal government during the thirties. It was not necessary for us to "spend and spend, tax and tax, elect and elect." It was not necessary for us to drop atom bombs on the Japanese. It was not necessary for us to encourage the communists to take over in China—or in Cuba. It was not necessary to send billions upon billions of dollars overseas with the end effect of strengthening our enemies. It is not now necessary for us to set up a compulsory system of medicare or of federal aid to education. It is not necessary to continue a grandiose program of farm subsidies that even the farmer does not want. It is not necessary to cease nuclear testing, to disarm, or to put ourselves at the mercy of the communist military power.

When we do what is not necessary, the ultimate result is divisiveness. The liberals, who are committed to this philosophy, have done well for themselves. They built up an ideology of power between 1912 and 1932, put it into use in 1933, and maintained it until 1964. But the sands upon which that system was built have shifted. The same economic, religious, and racial forces that were so instrumental in keeping the liberals in power are now breaking down that power. The result is rapidly emerging: a divided and a leaderless people.

And why does the liberal want so desperately to change things? Is it really because he has clearly thought out something better—or only because he is unhappy? Is there any assurance that changing the externals will make him any happier?

For all these years, the liberal has been in control. But read any liberal book, and determine for yourself whether the happiness of the liberal has increased. If anything, he is more sad. Galbraith and Schlesinger, for instance, constantly complain about the modern American world of advertising, television, tailfins, private profits, affluence. That world makes a colossal mistake in referring to the conservative as the reactionary one. Almost all the liberal does, it seems, is to react against the world he is living in. And, at worst, the conservative endures, feeling assured that the world of the present bears within itself the seeds of a better future—which may or may not germinate, depending on the character of future man.

Only that government can preserve freedom that limits itself to doing what is necessary, rather than trying to be all things to all men. Only that government is really a government of hope that is based on the experience of the past and on thanksgiving for the present. Only that government can unite that anchors itself to what *is* as everyone can agree, rather than to a multitude of opinions about what *should be*.

CHAPTER THREE

Economic Principles vs. Politics and Extremism

It was said, after the assassination of President Kennedy, that the election campaign of 1964 would be poorer, because, had Kennedy lived, his out-and-out liberalism would have been a fit foil for Senator Barry Goldwater's unvarnished conservatism. The campaign of 1964 *will* be poorer, because of the absence of Mr. Kennedy's vigorous and gracious personality. But a collision between Goldwater conservatives and Lyndon B. Johnson would provide even more contrasts than the more colorful, more dramatic clash between the senator and the murdered president.

In some ways, it would be even more of a head-on collision between liberalism and conservatism. For the liberalism of today's no man's land is not only a body of doctrine, it is also the quintessence of politics. The acceptance of life as politics* has become one of the most astounding and paradoxical features of modern liberalism.

In this book we have no hesitation in labeling Lyndon Johnson a "liberal," despite the fact that among conservatives he pretends to be a conservative. The modern "political" liberal, at least when he is standing for election or re-election, tends to take on the coloration of his surroundings. In 1960, Lyndon Johnson, as the liberal columnists Rowland Evans and Robert Novak

---

*The "other-directed man" of David Riesman's *The Lonely Crowd* is nothing but a pure politician.

acknowledge, made a speech to his Texas constituents denouncing the civil rights plank in the Democratic platform right after accepting the vice presidential nomination on that platform. L.B.J. ran for his Texas senate seat as a states' righter—if not a segregationist—and for United States vice president as a civil righter and integrationist.

Johnson is a champion of labor in union halls, and a spokesman for business at conferences of businessmen. He is a defense-through-strength man when speaking to veterans' organizations, and a pacifist and supporter of coexistence when appearing before the Americans for Democratic Action and kindred groups. He is even trying to blur the distinction between the Democratic and Republican parties. The President knows that his re-election depends on whether he is found out before or after the 1964 elections.

It was an accident that Mr. Johnson became president. But it is no accident that he is the kind of man he is. Liberalism, by 1964, had begun to run out of principles. The ones that remained were subordinated to political necessity.

This subordination is not congenial to the intellectual leaders of the liberals, such as Senators J. W. Fulbright and Joseph S. Clark, Arthur Schlesinger and Walt Rostow, Walter Reuther and Walter Lippmann. In 1964, indeed, liberalism was in its death throes, with the political liberals, such as President Johnson, willing to sacrifice conventional liberal impedimenta whenever it became unpopular, and the liberal intellectuals grimly determined to defend the last ounce of liberal doctrine.

At the same time, while a conservative such as Senator Goldwater could also be a politician, his principles came first. There was never any doubt where Barry Goldwater stood. Although the approach and the exact words were tailored to the audiences, the Goldwater message at koffee klatches, in sports arenas, in city and village, on the farm and in the union hall, at private conferences and at mass meetings, was always (1) let the individual, not government, do it, and (2) men (and nations) must be strong, not weak.

In fact, as time went on, Barry Goldwater kept becoming *more* conservative. In early 1964, as he began campaigning for the presidency, he discovered new dimensions to conservatism; for instance, even though a law on the books may begin as a liberal measure, it may come, by long use, very close to being a conservative one. As the senator began taking seriously the possibility that he might become president, he realized that any hasty change, no matter what was being changed, was closer to liberalism than to conservatism.

It is precisely this type of consistency that has gone out of liberalism. At one time, we repeat, the liberals had principles too—perhaps clearer than those of the conservative. Not so today. The liberal's "principles" are contradictory and opportunistic. Are we unfair? Let us see.

Principles vs. "Principles"

Principle, to the conservative, is fundamental truth, not simply a pious moral or ethical sentiment. For the conservative, a principle of human behavior or human conduct is both absolute and universal, in the same way that the principle of gravity is absolute and basic in physics. It operates from the inside, and is not superimposed by some external agent, whether human, governmental, or mechanical, even by the test of what men call "reason."

In *The Liberal Papers* David Riesman and Michael Maccoby note that "human reason, slender thread though it be, is the thread on which [all] our hopes hang." The conservative would dissent. Man's hopes depend, he would say, on principles. And principles, for the conservative, are not a "slender thread" but a toughly woven, strongly corded rope.

An example of a conservative principle is individual responsibility: the individual, when adult, must bear the responsibility for his own life and everything that happens because of that life. In many cases, this may be manifestly unfair and even unreasonable. A particular individual may be crippled, discriminated against, stupid or repulsive, or just plain unlucky. Or maybe, as in the book of Job, Satan is seeking to undermine him. But all this, the conservative philosophy would hold, is part and parcel of the individual in accordance with the Divine scheme of things. The individual must bear his own burden—and, of course, lighten it if he can. Conservatism is not a philosophy for sissies.

On the other hand, for the liberal, principles are based on, and hence clearly inferior to, reason and knowledge. Let us take as an example of liberal principle the statement "All men are equal." Liberals arrive at it by convincing themselves through a reasoning process that the obvious inequalities between men are not implied in the definition "man," and so are not basic. The liberal finds society, not the individual, to be responsible for these inequalities—perhaps by allowing some more money than others (as in the case of rich and poor), perhaps by providing better education for some than for others (as in the case of employables versus unemployables), perhaps merely by attaching a different valuation to some attributes than to others (as in the case of white versus colored).

While, however, the conservative principle of individual responsibility is absolute and universal, the liberal wants to limit severely the application of his principle of equality. While, for instance, he would be against discrimination between buyers or renters in housing, he would favor discrimination between sellers, as only some sellers would be affected by laws relating to selling to Negroes. When it comes to tax rates, or to restricting welfare handouts to those who can "qualify," or to directing federal agencies and others under the federal thumb to employ Negroes rather than whites, or in seeking to bar nonunion men from jobs, or to awarding defense contracts to "distressed areas" or other areas where gratitude would be most likely to be translated into support at the polls, or to ruling in favor of atheists and against Christians in public schools, or in preferring the theoretical over the practical man, or in dozens of other instances where discrimination would, according to the liberals, be dictated by reason, the liberal is "flexible" on the matter of equality. Truly the liberal concept of equality is more than meets the eye.

Nearly all liberal principles are similarly "flexible." They are not universal but relative to time, place, occasion, circumstance, political necessities. No wonder the conservatives, whose principles are fixed, find the liberals to govern and to be governed mainly by political expediency and opportunism!

Why are the principles of the liberal so flexible? Because they have to be—at least as long as the liberals hope to govern. If they were not, they would be revealed as a mass of contradictions. Even as it is, the contradictions of liberalism represent one of the fundamental facts of our time.

Liberalism Draws and Quarters Itself

The liberals are not willing to give up their claim to being sole owners of the four principles of "liberty," "democracy," "humanity," and "rationality." But with every passing day the four are increasingly in conflict with each other.

This fact is recognized by the more thoughtful liberals. In *The Liberal Papers,* for instance, Quincy Wright notes that the liberals are torn between "peaceful coexistence and mutual toleration," which "would seem to tolerate tyranny, regimentation and oppression, contrary to democratic values," on the one hand, and "freedom, democracy, constitutionalism, and progress," on the other, which "would seem to require non-recognition, propagandas [*sic*], and interventions maintaining high international tensions and cold war, threatening hot war likely to destroy mankind."

The greatest—and most fatal—conflict in liberalism is the one between its idea of "liberty" and its idea of "humanity." This conflict is inherent in the liberal's preoccupation with enlarging already Big Government in order to provide more welfare. Most liberals will acknowledge that government necessarily means coercion, and that this is inconsistent with their traditional objective of increasing liberty. Liberals have not been able to resolve this contradiction—except possibly on an *ad hoc* basis. Thus the liberals find that the liberty of white men must be restricted in order to promote equality for American Negroes, but that no pressure must be exerted on the free and independent new states of Africa in order to assure the white man of even an equal opportunity for life. And the liberals willingly give their permission for the overthrow of such governments as the Diem regime in South Vietnam, because of alleged oppression of Buddhists, while they resist any thought of interfering with the liberty of Castro, who is discriminating outrageously in favor of communists.

Almost as disastrous is the growing conflict in liberalism between "democracy" and "humanity." In almost every place a vote occurs on a civil rights measure, so dear to the liberal heart, the people turn it down. And there is no doubt at all that, if submitted to a vote, prayer in schools (which is said to discriminate against atheists and non-Christians) would carry overwhelmingly. Similarly the almost rabid liberal defense of foreign aid to increase the welfare of underprivileged countries encounters an overwhelming hostility and suspicion by the majority of American voters, which, incidentally, does not seem to diminish the modern liberal's enthusiasm for foreign aid in the least.

The most dramatic of the inner conflicts of liberalism, however, is that of "rationality" versus one or more of the other three concepts. The budget is a good example. The liberal intellectuals, who were rapidly taking over the places of power under President Kennedy, thought the unbalanced federal budget to be a positive good, and were even more interested in pumping money into the economy by the way of deficit spending than in using the spending power to promote welfare reforms. With the accession of Lyndon Johnson, the welfare-and-social-reform (that is, the "humanity") people climbed back into the saddle and began converting the original Kennedy tax-cut program into a piece of class legislation.

In education, the liberal intellectuals insist that federal money should never be given, or even loaned, to Catholic schools; the "humanity" liberals contend that children who attend parochial schools are just as deserving as public school children.

The "liberty" liberals have never quite resigned themselves to making agreements and deals with the communist tyrants. The liberal intellectuals, however, seem to be certain that anything that is good for Russia is good for the American people.

One of the most tenaciously held tenets of the liberal intellectual is anticolonialism. In this he is supported by the "humanity" liberal. It is a fact, nonetheless, that most of the newly-created governments of Asia and Africa have gone to fascism—of either the left or the right, as Barry Goldwater has put it. And fascism, liberals will admit, is undemocratic.

Liberals seem to agree on only two things: that they must stay in power, and that the country must be supplied with a "strong president." The only two objectives that liberals can deliberately agree on, that is, are political objectives.

Challenge to the Liberals

This is a harsh thing to say, especially about a philosophy with such a noble past. This book, therefore, issues a challenge to the liberals: Name a set of liberal principles, valid under today's conditions, that are (1) consistent among themselves, (2) workable in practice, (3) universally applicable, and (4) accepted by all, or nearly all, liberals. Conservatives can do this for their own creed. Can liberals? We, the writers, doubt it.

Today, liberals do not even stand unambiguously for peace and prosperity. If Russia were thought of as a fascist rather than a communist country, the liberals would almost certainly be as violently anti-Khrushchev today as they were anti-Franco during the middle thirties and anti-Hitler during the late thirties. And if some supernatural power were to solemnly promise permanent prosperity for all at the price of surrendering all the economic and social reforms since 1932, most liberals would refuse. Nor do they retain much tolerance or open-mindedness when really put to the test: that is, being tolerant of conservatism. The conservative himself, who makes no great claim to this virtue, is more willing than the liberal to listen to both sides.

The writers can think of only one liberal principle that is not honeycombed with exceptions: "I—and my peers—know best." Except for that, the liberal seems to be in headlong retreat from principle.

Liberal Extremism

This retreat from principle plunges the liberal into politics. It also plunges him into extremism. Extremism is a sign of nothing so much as a lack of inner principle.

One of the most bizarre efforts of recent times has been the propaganda designed to link conservatism with extremism. The two are utter opposites. In fact, extremism, in some senses, makes a better antithesis to conservatism than does liberalism.

The conservative, in thought, manner, dress, actions, is one who avoids the extreme, the excessive, the extravagant. Like Aristotle, the conservative seeks out the golden mean; like Plato, the liberal is entranced with the glittering, and often the sweeping, intellectual generality.

Nothing that is extreme can be conservative. If the John Birch Society is extreme, it is, *ipso facto*, not conservative. At the same time anything that is moderate *is* necessarily conservative. The reason? Because to be really moderate (as opposed to being merely bland), it must have a firm base in principle. And whatever adheres to undeviating, fixed principle—which, by definition, must be universally applicable and workable—is conservative.

"Principle," says Webster, is the "essential or characteristic constituent, that which gives a substance its essential properties."

That is, principle is inner, indigenous. "Extreme," as the lexicographer points out, is derived from *exterus,* meaning "foreign." The extremist is one who sacrifices his native common sense and intuitions, as well as the traditions and conventions of his society, in the service of emotional orgy or intellectual sophistication. The extremist is the man, for instance, who knows *for sure* that Nikita Khrushchev is fooling when he says he will bury us. The extremist believes in unilateral disarmament because we have, he thinks, passed into a new age, where weakness, not strength, is the best guarantee of security and freedom. The extremist is the man who is willing to destroy our bombers and, in the absence of total disarmament, rely wholly on a rather unreliable type of automation—guided missiles—that a freak accident or piece of communist luck could put entirely out of commission. The extremist is the man who is contemptuous of the wisdom of the race as accumulated in parable and saw, such as Aesop's fable of the ant who was saved and the grasshopper who perished. The extremist is the man who is so sure of his own power to distinguish right from wrong that, like President Johnson, he does "not believe that there are necessarily two sides to every question." The extremist is the man who ridicules the Constitution as fit only for a horse-and-buggy age, or the Bible as a fairy story.

The extremist is a man who, in short, knows it all. This phrase may fit a liberal like Robert McNamara, Lyndon Johnson, or Arthur Schlesinger. It does not fit a Barry Goldwater. It doesn't fit any conservative.

The Two Types of Principle

Today, liberalism, extremism, and politics are in alliance. Together they face their common enemy: principle. Principle, in our civilization, is of two types: religious and economic. We cannot discuss the religious source of principle here; this would require a book by itself. Suffice it to say that the Judeo-Christian religions are firmly based on conservatism, and are indeed related to conservatism much as living is related to life.

Economics is the mundane counterpart of religion. The two make common cause to keep politics in its place. Both economics and religion regard the world as struggle—religion, at least in the West, as the struggle of the individual to attain salvation for his immortal soul, and economics as the struggle of the individual to attain welfare for his mortal body. Politics, unavoidably necessary in a limited way, tries to escape limitation and bring both salvation and welfare as gifts from an all-powerful government, which would of course make both religion and economics, in any fundamental sense, unnecessary.

The Conservatism of Free Enterprise

Business, the sparkplug of economic progress in the United States, is not necessarily conservative. Indeed, if the main characteristic of the liberal is his passion for change and innovation, business, in some eras at least, has obviously been prevailingly liberal, as this book has already intimated, and as many conservatives have noted. *But the principles are conservative.** The economic principles of conservatives are derived from the most basic conservative principle of them all: whatever is, is.

The conservative believes the world is held together, not by the planning and the machinations of man, but by the fact that it *was created* to hold together, with the centripetal tendencies being, on the whole, stronger than the centrifugal ones. For the conservative, the first duty of man is to observe and accept what *is*, rather than to plan and scheme what *should be.*

And when, in economics, the conservative seeks to observe what he himself is, he sees an individual who is—and who has to be—basically self-interested. Even if he likes to think himself altruistic, the candid conservative will have to admit that he is

*As are businessmen themselves. See Chapter 4.

altruistic for selfish reasons: because it gives him a greater sense of self-satisfaction to be altruistic than not to be. No man can get outside his skin. Initiative, responsibility, honesty, loyalty, generosity, self-sacrifice—all must spring from self-interest. Or, as the liberal might put it, from a desire to realize his own full potential.

The next observation the candid conservative makes is that an individual is a bundle of energy that strives. (The liberal blinds himself here too, because he sees man, not as energy, but as brain). And what does the individual strive against? Two things: nature and his fellow man. His strife against nature can be called the creating of order (even though it does seem occasionally to result in increased disorder). In economics this creation of order is the production of goods and services, which, to the extent that the individual himself benefits from his own creation, can be called "profits." And strife against his fellow man can be called "competition." Finally, to accomplish anything at all, the conservative knows there must be certain ground rules.

These four—self-interest, profit, competition, and implicit ground rules—form a tightly knit group of economic principles based on the conservative acceptance of things as they are.

Liberal "Economics"

"Liberal economics" is not really economics at all. The liberal contribution in economics—whatever it may be in politics—is strictly a negative one, sapping the economic principles of the conservatives.

Economically, the liberals are the party of unemployment. There are three causes of unemployment—and the liberal magnifies all three. The first is that an employer is not likely to employ men if their wages add more to costs than they add to productivity. The minimum wage law means that some who would be hired at $1.00 an hour would not be hired if they were barred from accepting less than $1.25 or $1.50 or $2.00. Employed, even at a low wage, they might be able to work their way up. But the minimum wage law makes them unemployables. Quantitatively more important, as union scales have soared under liberal encouragement, making workers in unionized industries the economic royalists of labor, it has become profitable for industry to accelerate its normal pace of substituting machines for men.

The second cause of unemployment is that a man does not go to work unless someone—himself or another—has taken the initiative to create work for him to do. And it is unnecessary to detail the ways in which the liberals in power, through taxes and otherwise, have discouraged initiative.

Finally, men do not go to work if they are not permitted to. By endorsing union shops and other forms of labor monopoly, the liberals cut off the source of livelihood of those who refuse to join the union or who, like Negroes and other underprivileged, do not stand in well at union headquarters.

Economically, the liberals are the party of high prices. High prices are a mark of the inflation engendered by liberal deficit spending. As a result, the cost of living in 1964 is almost twice as high as in 1929, itself a year of inflation. In the absence of inflation, the gains in technological progress would have been shared with the public in the form of lower prices, rather than with those lucky enough to command wages or some other form of income able to rise faster than the price rise. If prices today were as low or lower than in 1929, most of President Johnson's "poverty" families living on $3,000 a year or less would be considered well off.

As a matter of fact, the formerly bright-eyed liberals (now suffering from a hangover) haven't solved a single major problem: not unemployment, nor high prices, nor racial discrimination, nor declining industries, nor undeveloped countries, nor farm surpluses, nor low incomes, nor lack of education and skills, nor communism, nor war. Thirty years in power and not a single problem solved except *by* war! And now liberalism is breaking up as its minorities become hostile to each other and its basic principles are revealed as mutually antagonistic. And still it seeks to reign! How much longer will it take before the American people realize that liberalism and political supremacy over economics cannot solve their problems? In an age of automation and great uncertainties, the only alternative to a vicious circle of liberal unemployment leading to liberal inflation leading, eventually, to more liberal unemployment is (other than out-and-out government coercion) a return to conservative economic principles.

The Moral Basis of Prosperity

To put it another way: In the United States we are making all our problems—especially including unemployment, inflation, racial strife—worse by insisting that the economic system should be controlled directly by men, rather than through principle. Try as they will, these men, calling themselves "economic planners," simply cannot control properly, because they can't (1) get perfect information, (2) devise perfect plans on the basis of this information, (3) communicate these plans perfectly to those who have to execute them and direct a perfect execution, and (4) do all this before the situation changes enough to call for something very different. Liberalism, so flexible in politics, can succeed in economics only as a cult of perfection, which implies rigidity. On the other hand, conservatism, with its doctrine of individual responsibility, which can meet changes in conditions while still retaining its loyalty to fixed principles, is wonderfully adapted to the requirements of a complicated economic order.

By 1964, it had become apparent that, in wrestling with the economic problems of the twentieth century, man's unaided brain had met its Waterloo. The planners simply cannot cope with all the billions of details, lightning-fast shifts, problems and conflicts and personalities and bottlenecks. Not even money can do it;

money, we are beginning to realize, is a resultant, not a cause.

The final economic cause indeed may be something like old-fashioned morality. For confidence depends on morality, not on money. Men cannot cooperate with each other, nor compete with each other, nor even make a decision, until they have agreed on certain ground rules for which morality forms the basis. The acceptance of a moral code underlies purpose, honesty, business taboos, ambitions, the admissible and the inadmissible, and all the attitudes and modes of behavior of economic life. No one can have confidence either in himself or in others unless he has formed a realistic idea of what to expect if he does, or refrains from doing, certain things. Certainly a balanced budget, for instance, is a moral rather than merely an economic objective. Without a balanced budget, profits and the like as goals to strive for, there could be no real pattern of national economic action. Little by little, the forces pulling us apart would overcome the forces enabling us to pull together. Only the acceptance of common moral ground rules can lay the basis for economic confidence.

Indeed, morality may be the point at which economic principle meets religious principle.

CHAPTER FOUR

People and the Head-on Collision

A liberal is a person who wants to run the world according to an idea—preferably his idea. Furthermore, his conception of "idea" is likely to be quite narrow. For instance, he doesn't admit that conservatives have valid "ideas." It is not characteristic of liberals to like or dislike people for their own sake, but rather because of the goodness or badness of what they represent.

Albert Schweitzer once defined a humanitarian as one who puts people before ends. The liberal has always posed as a humanitarian but has never been one. It is the *idea* of humanitarianism, not humanitarianism itself, that attracts the liberal. The true humanitarians are likely to be conservatives, and for a very simple reason: because both tend to like people for themselves alone.

The Liberal and the Idea

Much misunderstanding has resulted from the liberal preoccupation with "idea." In the first place, the liberal has built "idea" into such a god that it has obscured his ability to recognize and work with people as people. In the second place, conservatives often become somewhat unsure of themselves when confronted with the liberal's superior at-homeness in the realm of ideas, while the liberal, who compensates for a personal feeling of insecurity by a supreme cocksureness of the rectitude of his ideas, is confirmed in his "superiority." And in the third place, with the liberal thinking in terms of "idea" and the conservative thinking in terms of "people," the basis both for the waging of head-on collision and for its misfiring is laid.

Liberals claim to have a monopoly of ideas. They do read more than conservatives. The latter may protest, but nevertheless this is a fact hardly worth debating. When the conservative is participating in or watching athletics, exploring or visiting or making a business deal, or perhaps making love, the liberal is likely to be busily reading. On surveys, liberals report they "prefer books to companions," "find reading more helpful than conversation," "prefer intellectual matters to athletics," "express themselves better in writing than in speech." On the other hand, the conservative has more of a tendency to like and enjoy people, and to get much if not most of his information from more or less informal contacts with them—often without suspecting it.

As a result, while the liberal is likely to know more about the latest ideas, the conservative is better grounded in people and why they behave the way they do. If the conservative tries to follow established procedures and customs, it is because he knows that these are the ways civilization, after thousands of years, has hammered out. The liberal, on the other hand, notes that these customs and procedures do not scintillate with the brilliance of ideas, and is likely to scorn them. On the other hand, the glittering plans of the liberals are likely to turn into fly-by-night schemes simply because the liberal, so enchanted with words and ideas, mistakes the basic nature of people.

Perhaps even more important, the concentration of the liberal on ideas and especially on ideas that can be stated in writing, teaches him to avoid the head-on collisions of everyday living. Like Karl Marx, the liberal is tempted to ignore the smaller conflicts and competitivenesses involving his responsibilities as an individual and a family man, in order to devote all his attention to the only head-on collision he cares about, that of ideas, which in Marx's case was "proletariat" meeting "bourgeoisie," dialectical materialism meeting and overthrowing the Christian God, the nation-states that had been so unappreciative of him crushed and molded into a Communist International.

In the eyes of the conservative the liberal's preoccupation with ideas about people blinds him to people themselves. This could be so regardless of what the ideas are. But it is mostly likely to be the case when the basic ideas of the liberal turn out to be false. And this is what is happening now.

Darwin, Marx, Dewey, Freud: Pro-Liberal

Liberalism, as we have said, dates back to the Renaissance. But modern liberalism owes its form to four nineteenth-century thinkers, two of whom survived into the twentieth century and even did most of their writing then. These four, the liberal has been saying ever since, destroyed the conservative's idea of God and man. They are probably responsible for the liberal's conviction that the conservative is idea-less. The New Deal and the New Frontier were but the culmination of the thought of these men—or what the liberals interpreted as their thought.

Under this interpretation Charles Darwin (1809–1882) "proved" that man was not created by God, or at least by the kind of God Genesis seems to tell about, but rather evolved from lower animals. Furthermore, Darwin set up a mechanism to explain evolution—which included natural selection, sexual selection, mutations, direct effects of the environment, use and disuse —putting what had hitherto seemed mysterious into the comprehension of man's reason.

Karl Marx (1818–1883), honored not only by communists but by all modern liberals, showed that man has it in his power to build a better society, one that would not have the defects of the social order that conservatives had tacitly assumed had the blessings of God. Marx called his system "scientific socialism." He, too, provided a mechanism—the "revolution of the proletariat," the establishment of utopia, and the administration of anarchy (or perfect freedom).

John Dewey (1859–1952) showed that man not only did not need religion, he did not even need any *philosophy* that sought to transcend human experience. Dewey contemptuously dismissed the need civilized society had always felt for absolute values, and found "authority," at least as it had been traditionally understood in religion and education, to be quite unnecessary. The Dewey "mechanism" was education without any definite curriculum but under which the development of the child would be allowed to flower as he followed his own inclinations, children being born with a "*natural* desire to do, to give out, to serve."

Sigmund Freud (1856–1939) found the individual to be in conflict both with himself and with his culture, obsessed with sex, acting compulsively and irrationally, wasting his energies through fantasies, dreams, complexes, phobias, infantilisms, and so on. The mechanism by which Freud rescues the wrecks we know as "men" is to persuade them to tell a psychoanalyst all about their private lives, on the assumption that in this process they will begin to understand themselves ("bringing the original wish impulse to clear consciousness"), and that to understand is to forgive.

All four of these men attacked, each in his own way, the idea that there is an unknowable or transcendent element that can affect human affairs. The liberal immediately welcomed each, and modified the going definition of "idea" so that, rather than destroyers of "idea," these men would be placed among its creators. He then intermeshed these newly sanctified ideas with liberalism itself, using them to buttress his case that man, racially, socially, educationally, and as an individual, either is advancing or can advance toward perfection—and without any "unnecessary assumption" of a supernatural Being.

Darwin, Marx, Dewey, Freud: Anti-Liberals

At first these four men fitted nicely into the liberal pantheon. But, as time went on, the liberal became increasingly uncomfortable with Marx and Freud. Marx, whatever his virtues, still was the father of communism, which after World War II gradually became less and less respectable even among the intelligentsia. Russian and Chinese communism were revealed as tyrannous, murderous, treacherous, and even anti-intellectual—and Marx suffered by association. Further study of Freud pointed up the disquieting fact that, although he did strike a potent blow for atheism and materialism, his revelations of man as controlled by nonrational forces would in the end destroy liberalism, which, as we have seen, is based on the frail premise of the supremacy of reason and intelligence. Furthermore, Freud raised a host of questions that could not be answered from the liberal point of view but could from the conservative. The "unconscious" that Freud made so much of, for instance, could be interpreted by the conservative as a device by which God commanded man for reasons known only to Himself. Then, too, Freud's tomfoolery about sex proved embarrassing to the liberals, whose philosophy certainly does not emphasize instincts.

But it was Dewey and Darwin who, in time, gave the most jolting blows to the liberals. The failure of Dewey's ideas on education cannot be blinked away. By 1963 his educational philosophy had been tried out for almost two generations. And largely as a result, as we have seen, today Johnny cannot read.

Charles Darwin—the man liberalism welcomed with open arms in 1859*—rose from his grave nearly a century later and delivered the *coup de grâce* to liberalism. Man may have "evolved" rather than have been "created," say those whose job today is to bring Darwin up to date, but his "evolution" is becoming more reminiscent of Christian beliefs all the time. An-

---

*Publication date of *Origin of Species*.

thropologists have not yet accepted the fall, but it seems likely they'll have to accept the parable of Cain and the part that murder played in the very beginning of the story of man.

Robert Ardrey, in his *African Genesis,* cites compelling evidence to indicate that man became what he is today because of his ability to use weapons. Rather than prehistoric man "discovering" how to make and use "tools" (which were mainly instruments for the destruction of life) because of his big brain, African research indicates that man was the result when weapon wielding developed more and more manlike qualities, including the big brain, in submen. Man's brain, then, is result more than cause.

It seems quite certain that future research in the anthropological field, which owes so much to Darwin, will complete the destruction of the liberal idea. The new knowledge being uncovered today supports conservatism, not liberalism. For instance, the acquisition of property is not a wicked device of capitalism to enslave mankind. On the contrary, it is one of the strongest drives known, not only to man since his earliest days, but far down into the animal kingdom. The male urge to acquire *Lebensraum* is stronger even than the urge to acquire a mate. On the other hand, the impartiality and neutrality that means so much to the liberal is unknown in evolution, where another of the same species is always either friend or foe, and to be treated as such. Again, the anthropologists are rapidly demolishing the theory of the welfare state through their findings that animals in captivity who are provided with free food, drink, sex, and protection—as well as space—can hardly be called representatives of the same species as their free brothers who are responsible for themselves and those under their protection. Too, equality is unknown in the animal kingdom, where some variant of a "pecking order" seems to be universal. Social position for both prehistoric man and for animals lower than man seems to be derived not so much from sheer strength and cunning (corresponding to the "brains" liberals worship) as from a comparatively mysterious life-energy the leader seems to have in greater abundance than the other members of the tribe, or pack, or flock, or pride, or gaggle. Even more universal among all life, both animal and vegetable, is the presence of purpose—suggesting that everything, including evolution, may be as it is, not because we are all part of a great accident, as the liberals seem to think, but because it is all part of a Great Design.

The Four Strikes on Liberalism

Even with the evidence from anthropology and the other sciences incomplete, liberalism is already like a pinch hitter in baseball who already has had four strikes called against him, but who, due to the partisanship of the crowd, the kindness of the umpire, and the patience of the other team, is still at bat. The four strikes against liberalism are—

1. Liberalism is not working out. In progressive education, liberal programs are leading to uneducated people. In the welfare state they are leading to irresponsible people. In economic planning they are leading to inflation, deficits, loss of confidence, coercion. And in international affairs they are leading to profound lack of contact with reality.

2. As we showed in Chapter 3, liberalism is becoming increasingly inconsistent with itself. It started out to promote freedom; today it is justifying dictation, pointing out that people must be forced to be free. It started out to promote equality; today it is advancing the cause of inequality, at least in the field of civil rights, by making people acutely conscious of the color of their skins. It started out to promote the brotherhood of man—and is finding that the only way, apparently, to do it is to create conflicts between countries, between groups, and between individuals. It started out as idealistic, and is today spawning almost pure materialism. It started out to promote peace—and has hung up the record of backing the United States into each of the three wars of this century.

3. Liberalism is being undermined by evidence produced by the very "spirit of free scientific inquiry" it has so long cherished.

4. Liberalism is leaving the liberal without any sure knowledge of what to do next. This fourth strike against liberalism is a restatement and a culmination of the other three. Because of his record of failure, inconsistency, and unreality, the liberal's sense of values and sense of direction, always fragile, is breaking down. The liberal is finding it harder to make up his mind about anything. Today he is often in a position of leadership, but he is finding it harder to hold things together: no sooner does he dampen down a fire in one part of his domain than another twice as fierce breaks out somewhere else. The problems of the world are growing, and, because he is no longer dedicated to inner values and principles more important than life itself, his ability —or even desire—to do something about them is shrinking.

Most of us are allowed only three strikes. The liberal is still clinging to his bat and resisting all efforts to move him even with four strikes on him. In reality his side has already been retired, but he has been shielded from this trauma-producing knowledge.

The Insecure Liberal

There can be little question about the word that best characterizes the liberal of our times. That word is "insecure." Because he is basically so insecure, living, as it were, on borrowed time, it is only logical that he should base all his ideas and programs on a desire to guarantee security. The liberal wants to take the risk—and the faith—out of living.

In social security he is not content with the risk-spreading features of conventional insurance. No, the liberal finds a risk in the possibility that, if left to follow their own judgment, individuals may not voluntarily take out insurance. The liberal therefore during the thirties insisted on the compulsory feature for old-age and survivors' benefits, and during the sixties on a compulsory medicare program. Government and other forms of national spending for the liberal comprise one grandiose effort to compel prosperity and make it secure; the liberal seeks to remove the risk attached to trust in private individuals and to faith that voluntary spending and saving can satisfactorily undergird our economy. The whole international scene is dominated today by the results of the prodigious efforts under Roosevelt to develop the atom bomb and so make the nation (and the world) secure, and by the conviction of the Kennedy-Johnson administration that security is possible only if all other freedom-loving nations, such as De Gaulle's France, Macmillan's Britain, and (formerly) Diefenbaker's Canada are tied to the United States' apron strings.

This obsession of the modern liberal with security is the keynote to his character. Security has become the objective of life with him, and he has identified freedom with it, harnessed reason and intelligence to the chariot of security, and tossed overboard the reins of individual responsibility. This bespeaks, of course, his basic lack of inner security—natural enough when one considers the liberal's unwillingness to allow that any agency higher than himself or his own creation can be entrusted with molding his security. It also underlies his reluctance to engage in the head-on collision; conflicts of any kind necessarily tear down the type of security that reason provides.

The Liberal vs. the Head-on Collision

The liberal cannot be expected to face up to the job of making a perfectly frank defense of the welfare state. What, when you come right down to it, *is* the welfare state? Why, it is first of all an abandonment of the idea that individual men and women can take care of themselves—and an assertion that an almighty state must now feed them, clothe them, house them, educate them, administer to their health needs, tell them when to do this and when to do that. Second, for this country, it is a tacit admission that money and material considerations dominate man's desires and needs. But can liberalism afford to accept a head-on collision along these lines? Even the most depraved character among us clings to the feeling that he must never permanently relinquish the hope of being his own man clothed in his own integrity again. So liberalism draws a smoke screen around the naked issues of the welfare state.

Communism? No liberal administration can be expected to say: "Our objective is the defeat of communism at home and in the world." Such a declaration would range the liberal against the whole battery of materialism, discontent, and class consciousness, which he thinks plays so important a part in his control of the six minorities referred to in Chapter 2. The liberal cannot afford either to expose or to attack his sources of power.

How about the liberal's attitude toward education? All his moves are in the direction of federalizing it, but he cannot acknowledge his aim even to himself, as to do so would reveal his all-pervading distrust of local initiative. The liberal doesn't feel that local school boards either know enough or care enough to discharge adequately so important a job as education—but could he reasonably be expected to say this out loud, much less uphold this point of view in public?

Fear, even more than distrust, is the dominant element in the economic policies of the liberal. He has no confidence in the ability of millions of decisions made by private businessmen and consumers to result in a sound and growing economy—unless they are guided by a small clique in Washington. But can he be expected to make a clean breast of the motives driving him to economic planning? Can he be expected to stand up on a public platform and say: "I do what I do, and I don't do what I don't do, because I am afraid . . . afraid . . . afraid"?

The Liberal vs. Action

In his avoidance of the head-on collision the liberal is helped a good deal by his preference for words over action. He can make much good-sounding talk that has little significance for action of any kind. But then, for the liberal, action is not the vital core it is for the conservative.

In their frantic quest for the good opinion of the world, the liberals show how much more they value words than action. Every move a liberal administration makes in foreign policy (and often in domestic policy too) is elaborately weighed for its effect on "world opinion." Action is taken only after the administration has first assured itself that such action can be aptly described and amply justified in words. The basis for inaction is equally words. After De Gaulle made his firm stand against Britain entering the Common Market on its own terms, the Kennedy liberals were nonplused, excited, and frustrated. But then some New Frontiersman thought of the phrase "period of pause" to describe Franco-American relations while the liberals were making up their minds what to do. Washington thereupon settled back with a sigh of relief that another crisis was over.

It is ironical that the conservatives are frequently condemned as the party of inaction, because this is actually the correct label to apply to the liberals. To be sure, if "action" is taken to mean introducing a bill in Congress and twisting the arms of the legislators in an effort to get them to pass it, liberals can be considered very "active." On the other hand, when action involves providing the people with leadership, or the accomplishment of international goals, or crucial decisions such as war or peace, the liberal simply isn't "in it."

The three areas where the American people desperately need leadership have to do with (1) the menace of communism, (2) the atom bomb, and (3) the restoration of confidence. In all three areas liberal administrations have flunked out. The common people were far ahead of the New Frontier in recognizing the danger of communism, and if this issue is being wielded by the conservative right as a weapon against the administration liberals, it is partly because the liberals have never revealed their own anti-communist program.

The possibility of nuclear destruction is surely one of the great facts of the second half of the twentieth century. It cannot be ignored. It must somehow be integrated into the lives and the understanding of the people. How does the threat of the atom modify the pattern of thinking and living and acting appropriate to the first half of the century? What must civilians do to adjust their thoughts and their lives to the atomic age? What is the promise of the peaceful atom? On these questions dead silence from Washington. The liberals just don't seem to realize that the practical philosophy of the man in the street must be stretched to include, and to integrate, this great fact. Indeed the liberals don't seem to know this meaning of "integrate."

Probably the most fatal form of inaction liberalism is heir to is the inaction that seems to paralyze liberals whenever great decisions are to be made. Our involvement in World War II resulted from such paralysis. Washington knew long before the Pearl Harbor attack that it was to be made. The Japanese were prepared to turn around if they were intercepted or if preparations were made to defend our installations. They attacked only after an inexplicable inaction gripped Washington and prevented it from sending news of the impending Japanese raid.

Similarly, President Kennedy allowed Cuban rebels, trained under President Eisenhower's administration, to stage a comic-opera invasion of Cuba, with tragic consequences—without taking action either to stop them from a suicidal attempt that could only destroy them and give the United States a black eye, or to provide the air support that alone could have made the invasion attempt effective.

This pattern of inactivity repeats itself time after time in liberal governments. Such a pattern of error is not accidental. Inactivity is characteristic of those who have been exposed to liberalism.

The Liberal vs. Reality

Why? The conservative's explanation is that the more one is infected with liberalism, the more he sees the world as something it isn't. The liberal insists the world is his oyster. It isn't.

A professor once worked out some questions to separate liberals and conservatives on the basis of their fundamental philosophy of life. While a full report has never been published, the little that has come out is instructive, especially the answers to some of the true-false questions. Here are five of the most significant:

1. You can't change human nature.
2. Duties are more important than rights.
3. People are getting soft and weak through so much coddling and babying.
4. The heart is as good a guide as the head.
5. Few people really know what is to their best interest in the long run.

Conservatives tended to agree with these and similar statements, liberals to disagree. The professor, a dedicated liberal himself, called those who agreed "extreme conservatives" while those who disagreed were just plain "liberals." The percentage agreeing with these five statements is shown below:

	"Extreme Conservatives"	*"Liberals"*
No. 1	73%	30%
No. 2	63%	32%
No. 3	68%	31%
No. 4	58%	22%
No. 5	77%	43%
Average	68%	32%

The survey was extremely biased in favor of the liberals. The professor in charge* seemed to regard "conservatives" as a type of interesting but repulsive specimen to be gingerly examined under the microscope. Nevertheless, in part, the picture of liberals and conservatives that emerges is a true one, especially when the raw data, rather than the professor's conclusions, are examined.

In particular, the answers to these five questions, no matter how well rigged they may have been, show the conservative as a man of humility, who is much more inclined than the liberal to acknowledge that (1) he cannot change what his Creator has laid out, (2) he should be thinking about what he can do for others (and for his country) rather than what they ought to do for him, (3) being pampered, getting his own way, and living off the fat of the land may not be what he has been put on this earth for, (4) God works in mysterious ways that perhaps his heart can appreciate even though his head cannot understand, and (5) just because you want a thing does not mean you should have it.

On the other hand, the liberal is shown as much more likely to swagger off in the conviction that he can do anything, even to changing what God has made; that *his* rights at least are more important than his duties (which, transmuted, become other people's rights); that it will certainly not harm *him* to be given all the good things of life; that *his* head is so good he does not need to consult his heart too; and that there really must be quite a few others who, like himself, know what is to their own best interest.†

*Herbert McCloskey, Professor of Political Science at the University of Minnesota.

†On this last question, note that it was the one liberals agreed with most. Probably, however, the liberals who agreed interpreted it differently than did the "extreme conservatives." The liberals were probably tempted to inject mentally the word "other" in the question between "Few" and "people" in order to make it a statement that seemed reasonable. We can only speculate that if the question had read "*I* always know what is to my best interest in the long run," the conservative would have been the one to have disagreed, while the liberals would have agreed almost 100 per cent.

As illustrated in this example, conservatives and liberals tend to *see* the world and human nature differently. The two indeed are different kinds of people—perhaps nearly as different as men and women. Reality to the conservative is not reality to the liberal.

The conservative cannot pretend to be able to prove by using his brainpower that his view of reality is the true one, and the liberal's view is false. However, for the conservative, a grasp of reality is shown by the ability of men and women to deal competently with life. And he doesn't think the liberal is proving to be competent or even sensible.

The Liberal vs. the Boss

Many years before the survey described above, an earlier one had been made to distinguish between religious conservatives and religious liberals. Religious liberals are basically the same kind of people as political liberals; religious conservatives are basically the same as political conservatives. This survey included questions such as the following:

1. Do you generally dislike being told how to do a thing?

2. Have you ever been made to feel antagonistic or irritated on account of the "bossy" way a chairman conducts a meeting?

3. Do you take the initiative in opposing such a person?

The liberals tended to answer with an emphatic "Yes!" to these questions. We are not told just how the conservatives answered, but the professor who wrote up the survey (another pronounced liberal) reported: "It is noticeable that liberals and conservatives differ in their relation to domination."

Now, conservatives do not think it is "domination" whenever their boss tells them "how to do a thing." Conservatives take the lead in fighting for freedom and independence, but somehow the conservative does not consider that authority, in whatever shape it appears, is a threat to his independence. He is likely indeed to have confidence in his boss, and that confidence in his boss's right to authority is likely to be the very thing that gives him self-confidence.

Herein lies the basic reason that the modern liberal is anti-business—and why the businessman is basically conservative. More than simply being a devotee of private property or of *laissez faire*, a businessman is a person who makes timely, correct, and voluntary adjustments to authority. Because of the increasing importance of authority in business, a twentieth-century manager, when put to the test, is basically more conservative than the nineteenth-century entrepreneur.

Resentment of all authority by the liberal makes it clear why he is so preoccupied with cooperation. We would be too if we were unable to accept the foundation stone of cooperation: the necessity for authority.

What the liberal is really trying to do is to get cooperation without recognizing authority of any kind, and when he finds that impossible he substitutes coercion.

Even though his actions belie his words, the liberal keeps on calling for "the cooperative society," feeling that in the end sole reliance on cooperation (instead of both cooperation and competition) will be possible because:

1. Man is inherently good and perfectible.

2. All that people with contradictory points of view (that is, those who feel the urge to compete) need to do is to allow themselves to be guided by the basic ideas of liberalism—which, after all, are the "right" ones.

The conservative finds these two assumptions rather silly. "Man," the conservative says, "is both animal and saint. As long as the animal part of his nature persists—that is, as long as he remains on this earth—all of him will not be 'good and perfectible,' but part will be given to evil, weakness, and folly, which the other part of his nature must perpetually guard against."

And the conservative is getting rather impatient with the liberal's constant pointing to such ideas as those of Darwin, Freud, and Dewey—and sometimes Marx—as "proving" the correctness of the liberal's position. "It is high time the liberal woke up," says the conservative, "and realized that science itself, which he admittedly got started, is now beginning to disown him."

But believing steadfastly in his assumptions, the liberal has always stood staunchly against anyone trying to tell *him* what to do. He continues doing this until the whole structure of society begins tottering. And then his grandsons settle, since some kind of settlement is then necessary, for totalitarianism—where slavery is as absolute as the absolute freedom that their liberal grandfathers insisted on.

The Liberal: Arrogant Complainer

How far this decay of liberalism has already progressed is for the reader to determine. We wish only to suggest a framework to use in interpreting the news and events of our time. But there is little doubt that the liberal, finding that his "solutions" do not work, is growing querulous. The more an organization is populated with liberals, the more friction and dissension it seems to suffer from; about the only type of organization liberals really do well in is the college and university, where each professor can be allowed to run his classes as he sees fit. Administrative work by liberals, as most businessmen and government officials know, usually gets snarled up in a tangle of personalities.

Conservatives, too, prefer to "dominate" rather than "be dominated." The ultimate basis for the head-on collision indeed is the conviction by two potential opponents that one of them, or the ideas and institutions it represents, is more qualified to dominate than the other. To decide which, the conservative says, the two sides will have to fight. And the conservative openly and joyously prepares for the fray, while the liberal prepares to duck.

This liberal propensity to duck is not entirely temperamental. It is intellectual also. "Why," the liberal asks plaintively, "should we fight to decide which is the correct answer to a problem when I already know? Besides, someone might get hurt."

Adding this all together, it begins to appear that the conservative has at least one quality apparently missing in the liberal. While the conservative tries with all his might to win whatever head-on collision he enters, when he loses he has the ability to accept the verdict with equanimity. If he should find himself low man on the totem pole, well, "you can't win them all." The reaction of the liberal is quite different. The world can't do this to him; he is worthy of better things; there is no justice.

The liberal, as we have said, thinks in terms of *should* and overlooks the *is*. When the liberal was in his prime, and when there was no doubt about the realness of reality, this was not such a bad trait. And, on the other hand, the readiness of the conservative to accept the *is* tended to delay salutary change.

But today, with the world almost literally drowning in change, the willingness of the conservative to accept the *is*, at least provisionally, furnishes a welcome respite, and builds courtesy and good manners. Because the conservative maintains simply that he is what he is, rather than that the way he thinks and acts is the way all people should think and act, he can be deeply prejudiced, as southern gentlefolk are likely to be, and yet not intolerant. And with liberalism having run to extremes, and with almost no one defending the validity of the *is* purely on the grounds that it exists and has therefore become, to a small degree at least, a part of the pattern of reality, the characteristics of the liberal seem to be more destructive than creative.

PART TWO

The Major Issues

CHAPTER FIVE

Communism

"Communist" is the name applied to countries such as Russia, China, and Cuba, where the lunatic left has come to power. It also describes the parties all over the world loyal to these countries. The results of communism horrify liberals as well as conservatives, but while conservatives blame communism itself for this, the liberals cite a wicked distortion of communism. Until comparatively recently, it has been difficult even to get liberals to denounce communism by name; if they had to denounce anything on the left they much preferred to use the name "Stalinism." To see why requires that we make a comparison of communism and socialism.

The conventional distinction today between "communist" and "socialist" is that, while both strive to attain the socialist utopia, the socialist uses evolutionary, and the communist revolutionary, means. This distinction has a grain of truth, of course, but it would be more correct to define communism as socialism plus power. There has never been, and will never be, a durable socialist government. Socialism, like liberalism, is constitutionally ill-equipped to wield power. When socialists are put in a position of power, and fully accept it, they willy-nilly start becoming communists or fascists.

There are only two techniques of wielding power: the one based on the conservative philosophy, which emphasizes tradition, duties, constitutionalism, and the difference in abilities and status between men; and the communist technique, which concentrates on coercion because its philosophy (socialism) is unworkable. Neither socialism nor liberalism, regardless of whether they are defined as identical or not, can stand power.

Another essay in definition is necessary before the liberal attitude on communism can be made clear. The liberal doesn't like communism, but he hates fascism. His ideology assigns fascism to one extreme and communism to the opposite one. He has been so persistent in developing this point of view that it seems likely to hang on even after liberalism itself has been routed.

Actually, communism and fascism are *not* at opposite poles. They are both totalitarian systems of oppression, exploitation, despotism, and sadism. Fascism, as Peter Drucker has said, is the next step after communism has proved an illusion. As a matter of fact, fascism replaces communism at the point where socialist theory (except for purely propaganda purposes) drops entirely out, leaving undiluted power. Fascism is not even a technique of power. It is power itself.

Ever since the French Revolution, and especially since the 1930s, liberalism has been fighting on two fronts: (1) against conservatism, and (2) against fascism. Human nature being what it is, these two enemies tended to fuse and the liberals came to regard fascism as an extension of conservatism. Actually, however, while the two poles of farthest opposition are not communism and fascism, as we just saw, they *are* conservatism and modern liberalism/socialism/communism/fascism. Conservatism is the only philosophy of management and government yet devised that can abstain from at least the threatened use of naked power. As we leave conservatism, we approach, first, liberalism, which refuses to recognize that there is such a thing as power; then socialism, which concocts a utopia where the state will "wither away"; then communism, which uses power to maintain a government nominally based on socialist theory; and finally fascism, which dumps the now useless impedimenta of theory.

The Plight of the Liberal

The desperate need of liberalism today is to deny a family connection with communism. The liberals can't do this on the grounds of theory. Both communist and liberal believe in the principle of the welfare state: from each according to his ability, to each according to his needs. Both believe in coexistence, and are willing (or even anxious) to sacrifice the codes of morality, the inner values, the spirit of competitiveness, and the other features of our civilization that have historically made men conscious of themselves as separate individuals. Both communist and liberal believe in the rights of atheists; it is remarkable how many liberals in this country accept Marx's declaration that "Religion is the opiate of the masses." And, at least in theory, both communists and liberals tend to favor centralization, with private enterprise yielding to government, the localities and the states yielding to Washington (or Moscow), and the national government yielding to a "supra-national" authority.

So the liberals try to make the differentiation between liberalism and communism in the following way: In the first place, communism is "extreme." In order to make it quite clear what they are driving at, the liberal theory of fascism comes in very handy there. It enables them to define communism generally in terms of the fancied antithesis between communism and fascism—and so to avoid embarrassing themselves by trying to show specifically how communism differs from the modern variety of liberalism.

Next, the liberals seek to show that since communism occupies the extreme position in their political spectrum, and since they themselves obviously are not communists, neither are they extremists, but rather sensible folk who may believe in the same utopia that communists believe in, but who want to reach it by moderate, gradual, sensible means.

Finally, the liberal attempts to demonstrate that ends are not particularly important, everything being relative and all. The important thing is the means, he says. "And look!" he continues. "There is just no resemblance between the means I want to use and those of the communists."

This argument of the liberals is undeniably ingenious. And we, the writers, do not presume to judge whether it is valid or not. It is enough for us to be able to point out that this liberal philosophy, which subordinates ends to means, is currently making the liberal's problem worse, rather than solving it. Because of it the liberal has no real policy on communism, no power to make decisions where a clear view of final objectives is required (as in Cuba, South Vietnam, and Laos), no ability to push through a just and effective program on civil rights or anything else; no real consistency or firmness, but rather is constantly hopping from one subject to another, from one side of the fence to the other.

An Idea or a Desolation?

On the issue of communism even more than on any other, discussion fails to enable the conservative and the liberal to understand each other. The liberal feels his opposite number is attacking the theories of communism, and more specially Marxism, which he himself, with his political interests in and intellectual acceptance of the principle of class conflict, has never entirely disavowed. And further, noting the conservative's concern over the domestic communist menace, the liberal is easily persuaded that the whole thing is a conspiracy to "get" him.

For his part, the conservative cannot understand how the liberal can view with intellectual detachment a cancer that threatens to destroy everything he holds dear. The conservative unqualifiedly both hates and fears communism. He is confident of his ability to face it down when it comes at him from outside, but he knows himself defenseless if communism should approach wearing the faces of his neighbors and government officials.

When the conservative talks about the "evil of Marx," he doesn't mean what the liberal thinks he does. He is likely to be unaware of Marx's specific ideas—of how Marx uses the theory of surplus value, for instance, or how he was influenced by Hegel. And if he were to learn all this, the chances are it wouldn't make much difference. The conservative is not even upset so much by Marx's doctrine of the class struggle or by his prediction of victory for the proletariat.

What really upsets him is his feeling that communism is synonymous with obliteration of all moral values, all standards, all the qualities of mind and soul and spirit that make man more than a highly intellectualized animal—or a super robot. In communism he sees the desolation of literal hell.

The Head-on Collision Between Freedom and Communism

The conservative theory, that man is only an agent for carrying out God's will, has made possible the greatness of Western civilization, even undergirding the accomplishments of the liberals, who could never fully accept it. Man in his own capacity deserved the good things of life, the liberals said. Man himself was good, the liberals said, and so the more he knew, the more he had, and the less he was constrained, the better. There is no need for freedom to continue its gradual evolution, the liberals said. Let us now have it all at once, they said.

Little by little, the liberals began winning. They began putting their thinking into effect. At first, especially in physical science, they seemed to be marvelously successful. The more man knew, the better things *did* seem to be.

Today we have reached the culmination of the liberal line of development. In science, the ultimate is the atom bomb—for which the liberals have not been able to, and will not be able to, find a defense. They even seem to lack the will to try. In government, the ultimate is communism (and its astral self, fascism)—again, against which the liberals are powerless.

Both communism and the atom bomb were developed in the name of bringing about greater freedom. But they have become, jointly and separately, the greatest enemies of freedom. They threaten to reverse the whole thrust of a billion years of evolution.

Things have gone so far that it may, at least from the liberal point of view, already be too late, either for conservatism or for man. But in the conservative philosophy it is never too late. The consistent conservative would say that, nuclear war or no nuclear war, the world and the individual will last just so long as God decrees, and no longer. The conservative would have us, while continuing and redoubling our opposition to communism, the anti-Christ, give up our exaggerated respect for it. For, in the last analysis, if we are destroyed it will be neither the communism of some foreign land nor nuclear blasts that will do it. If we are destroyed, the agents of our destruction will be ourselves.

The highest freedom is to accept the world as the one God has made. Communism, in denying God, wars on this freedom in the same way that paranoia wars on mental stability.

CHAPTER SIX

One World Adrift

"The dominant theme in American international policy for a long time," observes Professor Charles E. Osgood in *The Liberal Papers*, "has been peace through strength." The professor then asks: "Is our security increased by this policy?" No, he answers his own question, it isn't. Instead it is an "intolerable state of affairs."

We may not agree with Professor Osgood as to the intolerability of the peace-through-strength policy, but we do agree that this policy has been challenged, and that the cleavage between liberal and conservative on foreign affairs is becoming extremely sharp. If the liberal would stand still and not duck, it would be an outright head-on collision.

With the traditional American policy of strength under attack, the military, and the conservatives generally, are leaping to its defense, rechristening it the "victory" policy: The opposing policy is probably best known as the "peaceful coexistence" concept, first enunciated by Nikita Khrushchev. In the United States, peaceful coexistence seems to be identified with the names of Senator Fulbright, the Americans for Democratic Action, and the rest of the Liberal Establishment. Both grand strategies have been labeled by their opponents as "extremist," but are rapidly becoming typical of rank and file liberals and conservatives.

Since the United States has followed the "victory" policy in the past, and since the adoption of the coexistence theory would be a departure from it, let us first see what that one means and what its advocates have in mind.

Why Not Victory?

To Americans "victory" has been the objective of long standing. "Victory" was certainly our aim in the establishment and preservation of the American union, and the goal of American foreign policy (though tempered a bit in World War I and a bit more in World War II) down to the Korean War. "Victory" has been the objective in all our election campaigns, local, state and national; in all our numerous crusades for social justice and against graft and corruption; in the privations, determination and heroism involved in winning the American West; in the careers of millions and millions of individual Americans in overcoming obstacles and handicaps, and making a living for themselves and their families.

"Victory," when all is said and done, simply means clarifying a purpose and carrying it out against hardship and opposition. Webster uses head-on-collision language: "Victory" means "the overcoming of an enemy in battle, or of an antagonist in any contest; conquest; triumph;—the opposite of *defeat*." "Victory" is "overcoming of an enemy or of any difficulty," adds Funk and Wagnalls. "Any hard-won *achievement, advantage,* or *success* may be termed a '*victory*'."

"Victory," then, means "success." And we are sure that any person with common sense will acknowledge that during all the years since Columbus discovered America down to Truman's cashiering of General MacArthur, success has been officially, and personally, the American objective. In fact, the goal of success has been pursued since the arrival of civilization on this globe, and probably since the first amoeba swallowed the first bacterium.

It is no wonder that conservatives are thrown aback by the need to make out a case for victory—not only that we *can* fight and win, but that we *should.*

The excuse for the attempt by the liberals to bring about reversal in the historic policy of humanity is, we know, the atom bomb. "Victory," the liberal, who dislikes the head-on collision in any form, has convinced himself, means nuclear war, and an American policy leading toward war (except a war against fascism) the liberal finds to be unthinkable. "Victory in war, even if we were able to wangle such a thing," the liberals say, "would be the same as defeat."

The conservatives agree, of course, that a nuclear holocaust must be avoided. Neither side could be said to "win" or "succeed" in an all-out nuclear war. Those who urge the "victory" concept are now, and have been for generations, on the side of peace. The spiritual forebears of the present generation of conservatives include many who fought against our involvement in World War I and World War II, and many of today's conservatives themselves played an important part in settling the Korean War.

Why Not "Inevitability"?

"Peaceful coexistence" was raised to the rank of a grand policy by Khrushchev in an article in *Foreign Affairs* for October 1959. Probably its best definition appeared in the newspaper *Soviet Russia:*

"Peaceful co-existence is the general line of the foreign policy of both the U.S.S.R. and the other socialist countries. This does not mean, of course, peace in the class struggle between socialism and capitalism or reconciliation of the communist with the bourgeois ideology. Peaceful coexistence means not only the existence of states with different social systems, but also a definite form of class struggle between socialism and capitalism on a world-wide scale. This form includes giving up military means for solution of controversial international questions and, at the same time, presupposes an ideological and political struggle and economic competition. Socialism need not resort to war for victory on a world-wide scale. Its ideas will inevitably win through peaceful competition."

This concept has proved very attractive to American liberals, and has been echoed in their writings. The prospect of socialism "inevitably" winning under coexistence adds to, rather than detracts from, the attractiveness. For the last thirty to fifty years, indeed, we have been edging into the "coexistence" (or weakness) policy. Under it communists and socialists have, in recent generations, made great strides. The communists captured Russia and China, as well as the satellites and Yugoslavia, and built up important communist parties in many countries. As this book went to press, they were winning in Africa and in the rest of Asia. The socialists captured liberalism in the United States, and through it the Democratic Party, built the Labour Party in Great Britain almost from scratch, and have been making ready to challenge for power in West Germany after Adenauer has been forgotten. The American liberals of today at least should be hyphenated as "socialist-liberals."

The communists have little respect for either the socialists or the "socialist-liberals," viewing them most often as dupes to outwit. On the other hand, the socialists seemed to have always entertained under their outward hostility a secret admiration for the communists, which often took the form of a twisted expectation that the communists, being reasonable folk, would shortly come over to socialism.

When Khrushchev offered the peaceful coexistence policy, the United States socialists (parading as liberals) were overjoyed. "Now," they thought, "Russia is at last beginning to shed its disguise of communism and we can have an honest-to-goodness socialist one world." They realized it would be too much of a shock for Russia to disavow communism all at once, es-

pecially with China already on her back. Khrushchev's offer alone
was good enough for them. It only remained to get the United
States to respond in kind.

"The Communists Are Mellowing!"

For the American liberal, Khrushchev's expressed desire for
peaceful coexistence was proof positive that the communists were
mellowing. In fact, for years the liberals have been writing these
glad tidings in books and articles and secret reports to the White
House; shouting them from public platforms; seeking (and often
succeeding) to mold American foreign policy to conform to
this new doctrine of salvation.

The American liberal has been detecting a liberalization of
communism ever since the Russian Revolution. Such detections
tend to cluster around the time of Roosevelt's recognition of
Russia in 1933; the popular-front agitation of the later 1930s; the
World War II lend-lease generosity to Russia; the various postwar gifts of territory and influence to Russia, sometimes called
the postwar treaties; the death of Stalin; the retirement of Malen-
kov; the accession of Khrushchev. And now Khrushchev has come
through with "peaceful coexistence"! The communists have been
bountifully rewarded for projecting this mirage: billions in lend-
lease aid; permission to grab German factories, machinery, and
scientists at the end of the war; Poland and East Germany ceded
to Stalin in the Yalta and Potsdam agreements, the former of
which also gave the communists a base for their conquest of
China; the American help given the communists and withheld
from their enemies while they took over China and Cuba; the
billions in American foreign aid that went to strengthen the
communist cause, and so on.

Needless to say, the communists themselves, as always, tend
to see the coexistence gambit in a different light. Unlike the lib-

erals, the communists do not run to looseness of lip, except when it is to their advantage. However, Khrushchev, who seems to have entertained a good deal of respect for the late American poet Robert Frost, may have come close to leveling with him when the poet paid a visit to Russia in 1961. He was quoted after his return as commenting that during an hour-long talk with Khrushchev the communist leader "said he feared for us because of our lot of liberals. He thought that we're too liberal to fight. He thinks we will sit on one hand and then on the other."

President Kennedy said he doubted that Khrushchev said *that*. According to an article by Walter Trohan, in *Human Events*, the American president felt that the poet had made the remark and that Khrushchev had only agreed with it.

Going Deeper

In spite of all their professional dodging, the evidence is growing that liberals are a gullible race. *Why* are they so gullible?

The answer seems to be twofold. First, their insistence that people are innately good and perfectible, and that the only evil is that produced by "conditions." And second, their lack of experience in the ways of the world—the leaders of the liberals being professors, bureaucrats, rich men's sons, and scientists, in that order. And the two causes keep reinforcing each other.

Liberals do not know people. They know a lot of ideas about people, but they have never had the experience that could enable them to feel these ideas in their guts. And every time some experience starts coming their way, they insulate themselves from it by seeing only what their doctrinaire liberalism tells them to see. As apparently both Khrushchev and Robert Frost divined, most modern liberals have never fought for anything in their lives, which have generally been placid, with perhaps a few temper tantrums but no real evil. Few liberals have ever been pressed into situations where the only way out would have entailed hurting someone. The liberal is inclined to dismiss morals lightly as a particular kind of tribal custom, because his own personal codes of conduct have probably never been deeply challenged, and he has never had a real need for fixed and firmly based standards of morality. Your typical liberal may have been burdened with a few unpleasant chores from time to time, but no back-breaking responsibilities. Very scarce indeed has been the liberal experience comparable to that of an army commander before battle, who knows he is certainly sending some men, and perhaps a regiment, to their death.

The gullibility of liberals is not due to low intelligence. On the contrary, liberals tend to have high IQs. If they are suckers, and we think the record shows they are, it must be the lack of experience and thinking that makes other men acutely conscious of the reality of life.

The Dream of Weakness on a Par With Strength

Instead, the liberal dreams. While the history of liberal administrations has been a history of gullibility, dreams, and the dodging of reality, "dreams" is the key word. Congressmen, editorial writers, and representatives of the people can talk and write until doomsday about the inadequacies and evils of the foreign-aid disease, but their arguments will never make an impact upon the really convinced liberal. For the liberal is concerned not with facts but with preserving the dream of liberalism now threatened with destruction—a dream of how the world *should* work, and that it *can* be made to work this way.

Barry Goldwater once pointed out that a weak nation will thumb its nose at a strong one whenever it thinks it can do so with impunity. The liberals were horrified. The whole thrust of their policy has been toward eliminating any suggestion that the ultimate deciding forces are strength and weakness.

"Reason, not strength," the liberals (who apparently feel they have a much surer grip on the former than on the latter) insist, "should be made the final arbiter." Few conservatives have any special desire to get into *that* argument. Conservatives are usually content merely to point out that, slice them as you will, the world's most important problems *are* settled by strength. And conservatives are not prepared to accept the United Nations, co-existence, One World, or any of the liberal's nostrums if it claims power to abolish the doctrine of strength. The conservative knows this is not possible, and that the most that can be done in this direction is to hamper the virtuous use of strength and so permit the vicious use of strength to prevail. And this is precisely what the conservative fears from liberal dreams.

Let us analyze the liberal dream of One World in the light of common sense, not simply to show that it *is* a dream (or a nightmare), but to better understand how the liberal thinks, even in the daytime, and why the communist has such a low opinion of him.

United Grab Bag of the World

The starting point of the liberal dream is a United States of the World—with a communist USSR, a Hindu India, a Moslem Near East, and a Christian America and Europe owing much the same type of allegiance to what James Warburg, in another *Liberal Papers* essay, calls a "supra-national world organization," that the thirteen American colonies owed their federal government in 1789—except, of course, that there would be no constitutional guarantee of a republican form of government, no Bill of Rights (at least not one expected to be taken seriously), and none of the other features of a rule of law.

Instead, the communist states would be huge monopolies of political and economic power, with all property and all production centralized in the hands of the government. Neighboring democratic states, with their preference for private property and private enterprise, would be no match for the bargaining power of the communists, who, moreover, would be using their economic power for political ends. And at the same time the Christian states, loyal to a conception of truth and honesty, would try to keep their agreements, while the communist states, seeking to promote the dictatorship of the proletariat, would tear theirs up as soon as it became advantageous for them to do it.

As there would be similar, though less striking differences between Christian and Buddhist, Christian and Hindu, Buddhist and Hindu, and so on, the United States of the World would start out less auspiciously than the United States of America, which itself came close to breaking up several times, and once almost did. However, since the "supra-national police force" is likely to be drawn under the domination of the communist states, because the communists understand police affairs so much better, this problem is not likely to last long. A Gresham's Law would spread communism throughout the United States of the World.

"Nothing Is More Important Than Anything Else"

Let us repeat that the liberal is certainly not a communist, and seeks to prevent the spread of communism, rather than to promote it. But in foreign policy he is even more careless (and more dangerous) than in domestic affairs because he is, as Leonard Read once said, "adrift and without compass." The liberal has shucked his values; he substitutes dreams for reality; and he is hopelessly confused.

The liberal who used to talk so much about "human values" has decided that, after all, there is not much difference between values, and makes the outrageous proposal that communism and Christianity can be regarded simply as rival ideologies. At this point, the liberal's traditional devotion to "tolerance" enters the picture. The liberal emphasizes tolerance so much that it almost seems that he believes all things are of equal importance and equal value. Man must decide between his different ideologies by as rational a procedure as possible, the liberals say, adding, "after all, some may be communists, some Christians, and some of other sects and dogmas, but we are all people, aren't we? And *that* is the important thing."

The Conservative and One World

The conservative disagrees. To him the important thing is not that he is a human being, but the kind of human being he is. He is even likely to be more proud of being a Christian and an American than being a member of the human race. And he may object to being put in the same "One World" with communists, after being well entangled in commitments he cannot break without forfeiting his honor as an American and his obligations as a Christian, but which the communist cannot keep without becoming a "bad" communist.

Hitherto, liberal schemes have been saved from disaster by two facts: first, they have been incorporated into law, executed, and enforced in basically conservative America, which has always been able to temper them with a strong dash of common sense; and second, the proposals of the liberals in America have so far only had to pass inspection by men and women who were raised in the same tradition, who had a good deal of understanding and sympathy with the intent of the law, and who could see beyond the letter to the spirit. In other words, common values made the background one of faith as well as reason.

By enlisting the support of the conservative, it is possible that the One World scheme, too, may be saved. And his support may not be too hard to gain. After all, the conservative knows that we all live in the same world. Most conservatives will willingly admit that perhaps someday there *should* be a world government.

If world government is ever to arrive, judging from history, it would be brought about not by centralization, but by decentralization, that is, by mutual trust among the governed decreasing the necessity of coercive government.

When did the United States start becoming a united nation? Why, in 1776 and before, when it started breaking away from the centralization of the British Empire in order to assume responsibility for its own destinies. And Germany? Unification in 1871 was only the culmination of centuries during which the Germans learned to feel themselves a people apart from the Holy Roman Empire. Italian unification was similar. The great historical accomplishments of unity have always come about when the ties of administrative centralization have been broken and replaced by ties of kinship, common values, and mutual interests —not when they have been welded through a mere preference for "togetherness." When the time is ripe, One World too will well up from the bottom, not be imposed from the summit.

The liberal, of course, wants One World now. He calls attention to the possibility of nuclear war. "We can't wait," he says. "Only One World can prevent war." The conservative would agree that peace and One World are related, but would realize, even if unconsciously, that the peace we need so desperately today, even in this atomic age (or perhaps better, especially because of this atomic age) is the peace of the human soul, not the peace of men sitting around a conference table each thinking to himself what an S.O.B. his neighbor is. The conservative, as always, is suspicious of the glib, mechanical "solutions" the liberal dreams up. "The liberal," his opposite number thinks, "surely must have learned by this time that the most bitter and bloody wars are civil wars, and that the kind of administrative coercion that would be necessary to keep a Union Now world government together simply does not lead to genuine friendship and understanding." Mere physical, economic, and political proximity, the conservative knows, does not mean brotherly love. There is more hatred today in the age of the jet airplane, where nearly every spot in the world could be brought within twelve hours' flight distance from every other spot, than ever.

Speculation Over Liberal Backbone

The coexistence policy, it is safe to say, plays into the hands of the communists, and it actually delays the accomplishment of a true One World. But these are not the only liabilities the liberal, when conducting foreign policy, has to contend with.

On the face of the matter, considering how easily he is led, it would appear that the communist would like to deal with the American liberal. And so he does—up to a point. But, as the liberal himself is so fond of pointing out, communists are not necessarily any more enamored of the idea of dying in a nuclear war than people with a lot more to lose. And while Khrushchev, say, may have a poor regard for the liberal's backbone, he knows that liberals are especially prone to temper tantrums, and that while he would probably be able to get away with murder if he plays his cards right, he never knows when the liberals will unleash war over a relatively small theft.

Furthermore, when Khrushchev negotiates the Russian leader is, to some extent, two persons. He is both the head of a communist party and state, and a man who could be deposed and executed tomorrow. Communists have always played for high stakes, and have always tended to look down on socialists and liberals who do not. Rightly or wrongly, the communist inclines to the opinion that the socialist/liberal does not know what he wants, and is reluctant to treat him as an equal. Rather, the communist must, to a certain extent, regard the liberal as one who could put his neck in a noose if the latter undergoes a change of mood.

It is likely that communists know that conservatives *do* have final aims and final values, and that because of this conservatives can be trusted. It is even possible that a communist leader might betray his own people in dealing with a conservative, but with a liberal he would be afraid that he would be the one to be betrayed by some indiscretion the liberal would make.

Observing the development of liberal foreign policy in the United States as it is reflected in the giveaway of China, Laos, Katanga, Cuba, and other bastions, as well as the apparent American cheerfulness in allowing foreign-aid money to be used in financing America's enemies, and the proclivities of the liberals in undermining and trying to undermine friendly governments in Canada, Britain, Belgium and France, Khrushchev can hardly be blamed if he refrains from coming to any terms with a government that, in the case of liberal indiscretions, could destroy him.

For the communist to wangle concessions from a conservative American government dedicated to the "victory" or strength policy would be rough, and all those in or near power in Russia, China, and the other communist countries, together with many of their supporters, know it. A Khrushchev would therefore not be subject to a barrage of criticism for not pulling off another Yalta or Potsdam or Cuba or Laos in his dealings with a conservative president. But with the coexistence-prone liberal? No communist knows the extent of the concessions he may reasonably expect from a liberal United States government. Therefore, to retain power, the communist chief will tend to press for more and more, until, combined with the liberal's temperamental instability and penchant for confusion, he pushes the world close to war.

Most of the wars of the twentieth century have come about in this way.

CHAPTER SEVEN

Individual Gumption, or Welfare State?

The demand for a welfare state comes when a people no longer have the gumption for the head-on collision. This is what happened both in Germany and America in the early thirties. The gumption was drained out of both countries—though for very different reasons. And the people, both in America and in Germany, abdicated to the government.

On January 30, 1933, Adolf Hitler became chancellor of the Reich. A little more than a month later, Franklin D. Roosevelt became President of the United States. The differences between the programs they inaugurated were vast. But both held that their respective countries were entitled to more welfare—and that nothing should stand in the way of their getting it. This joint passion for welfare is more significant than the fact that each defined it differently. Roosevelt, in common with most of his countrymen, tended to think of welfare as consisting of a series of rather definite specifics: money, food, health, good housing, a car or two, "gracious living." The Germans, on the other hand, thought of it as a subjective state resulting from feeling prosperous, fortunate, able to express themselves, looked up to by their neighbors, superior to others. If carried far enough, it is obvious, this second list could become pretty extreme—and Hitler was the ideal *Fuehrer* to make it extreme. And for both American and German, this tendency, in the one case to prefer the particular and in the other the abstraction, was aggravated by the conditions prevailing in 1932 and 1933.

Background for Welfarism

Since 1918, Germany had been living in the shadow of war—partly past war and partly future war. The Weimar Republic was identified with defeat, surrender, and weakness. Militarily, Germany had adopted the fiction that it had lost, not because its army was beaten, but by "a stab in the back." Politically, Germany was schizophrenically divided between extremes with little popular support for her constitutional government. Financially, the German people were first jolted from reality by the hyperinflation that had reduced the mark to a value of 4.2 *trillion* to the dollar, wiping out their savings and wrecking the classes of greatest stability, and then enabled to live in some comfort, until 1929, by a constant stream of American and British loans. And after the crash, economic reality, with its six and a half million unemployed in 1932, following so soon the extravaganzas of war and peace, seemed too brutal to be borne. Germany deserved better! And the words of Hitler salved the wounded German spirit. In the same way, the words of Franklin Roosevelt also offered balm to his people.

In sharp contrast to the Germans, the Americans had, before 1929, an unbroken record of success. Victory in World War I and unprecedented prosperity during most of the twenties for most of the people added to a long history that seemed to justify boundless optimism. Even more to the point, we had come to feel that success and prosperity, rather than symbols of God's unmerited blessing, were the right of a deserving nation.

Therefore, when depression descended, it provided a shock that no previous economic decline had ever done. For one thing, a constantly increasing importance had become attached to material prosperity. For another, the transition from rural to city life, accompanied by the more profligate and less self-reliant habits of the city dweller increased vulnerability to general economic reverses. In the third place, since uninterrupted prosperity had become accepted as normal, a departure from it was coming to be regarded as an affront to man's rationality and ability to control his own affairs. And finally, with the American's uneasy dislike for abstractions and universals, almost the whole of his attention was held by the disjointed and unabsorbed present.

Nazi and New Dealer

Normally, people experience a continual head-on collision between thoughts and things: a head-on collision that enables them to keep their mental balance, aware of the importance of both. By 1933, however, most Americans, under the spur of privation and insecurity, had begun thinking only about things; and the Germans, blaming their troubles on the Jews, and anywhere else but on themselves, were becoming oblivious to facts and thinking only about thoughts. Fitting in with this development in national temperament, while both National Socialism and the New Deal contemplated a comprehensive program of social security and other measures for the material welfare of the people, in the New Deal this was an end in itself, but in National Socialism simply a subordinate feature in a program designed to provide welfare for the national soul.

This difference in the psychological characteristics of the two nations has concealed the fact that Nazi Germany was just as much a welfare state as New Deal-Fair Deal-New Frontier America. Indeed social security was given its start in Bismarck's Germany as a device—not too dissimilar to its role in Naziland—to keep the populace contented and amenable to the grand designs of the state.

Both Nazi Germany and New Deal America abandoned the philosophy of the head-on collision when they went to the welfare state. Whatever the particular brand of welfare state, it eliminates the thousands and millions of small head-on collisions in the form of countless competitions and conflicts. But since the head-on collision represents a deep-seated human need, the welfare state creates an *ersatz* one: the "struggle" against the Jews in Hitler's Germany; the "struggle" against the "economic royalists" in Roosevelt's America.

And, allowing for the differences between play acting and the real thing, the role of the "economic royalists" in the United States was curiously similar to that of the Jews in Germany. Both countries needed a scapegoat to explain depression, unemployment, frustration, and the restlessness and dissatisfaction of spirit that the welfare state always brings with it. And in neither welfare state could the administration, once it had taken its stand on the identity of the "villain," extricate itself.

Welfare states need a public enemy upon which the righteous can pour their wrath.

What Is the "Welfare State"?

A welfare state is not merely a batch of apparently humanitarian legislation, such as old-age and survivor's pensions, unemployment compensation, minimum wages, medicare, aid to dependent children, and the like, any more than it is Jew-baiting, "health through joy" labor camps, planned recreation, goose-stepping organizations—or, for that matter, bread and circuses.

The essence of the welfare state is that the state pretends to know what the welfare of its citizens calls for—and has appointed itself the provider of that "welfare." Before, "welfare" was something between individuals, or at most between an individual and a small group, perhaps in its implications not too different from "love" or "loyalty"; now, it was to be handled on a vast, impersonal, organized basis. Before, the family and the individual were the units of responsibility, and the citizenry guided, protected, and financed the state; now, the state accepted responsibility for the "welfare" of its citizens and for their guidance, protection, and financing. Before, initiative came from individuals, and the state was simply a vehicle reflecting that initiative; now, the state was to be the spark plug, devising the doctrines and the slogans (even when they seem most "liberal"), and the citizen was to be "free" from all the unsettling and necessitous conditions that give rise to initiative.

It would be a mistake to suppose the welfare state was a conspiracy to make slaves out of free men. Quite the reverse. All welfare states are set up by sincere men who want to do good. Hitler and Bismarck and Caesar were "good" men in this sense, no less than Roosevelt and Kennedy were. They all try to do their best for "their" people, according to their lights. The possibility that their "lights" may be defective is, of course, the hazard of the welfare state.

The Conservative and the Welfare State

The welfare state is utterly a liberal contrivance. The liberals, who believe that sincerity and "goodness" are much the same thing, and that men are "good" (and sincere) unless conditions make them "bad" (and insincere), can see no reason why the machinery of government should not be used to help the people to an easier and a better life, at least when it is financially and economically able to do so.

The liberal will grant that administering such a welfare state opens up a host of problems, but given good will and knowledge of how to go about tackling them he sees no reason why they should not be solved. After all, when the philosophy of the welfare state takes over, "economic royalism" and the other sources of corruption will have been overcome.

The conservatives do regard the "problems" opened up by the welfare state as insoluble. They see man as mixed good and evil, with the evil needing to be constantly kept in check—and they see the welfare state as removing these checks. On the one hand, the welfare state gives its administrators almost untrammeled power over the life of the individual; without checks and balances, the conservative believes, this power will corrupt them. On the other hand, the individual who is given "welfare" simply for the asking (or even before) loses his sense of responsibility and his appreciation of cause and effect, the conservatives say, and he too will, in time, be spoiled and corrupted.

The conservative sees society as a finely woven fabric all the threads of which the welfare state begins to rot. The mutual pressures and linkages of traditionally organized society keep individuals "straight," in his opinion. When the welfare state tells individuals, in effect, that they can do whatever they want to do, not only does society begin disintegrating, but the individual, as a civilized, Christian being, also disintegrates.

Power and Duty

The liberals think of the welfare state as humanitarian. To the conservative it is sheer, unadulterated power. "Power," the conservative, if he thought long enough, would define as "one's ability to do whatever he wants to do" unconstrained by duty. And by "duty" the conservative, unlike the liberal, would not mean "what one *thought* was his duty." No, this would be getting right back where he started. Duty, the conservative would maintain, is made clear to one independently of what he thinks about it—perhaps by a head-on collision; perhaps by the way life actually works out; perhaps by the laws, traditions, and customs of his society, which he accepts without thinking about them; perhaps by his religion. The researches of the liberal have shown that most so-called thinking is really only what one *wants* to think. The liberal calls this "rationalization," and it is high time that the conservative awoke to the implications of this finding in bolstering his own position.

By no type of intellectual ratiocination, the conservative maintains, can one put a check on one's lust for power. This lust creeps up on a man without his being aware of it. Only by using resources outside one's brain, forces of society, of education and training, of tradition and custom, can man contain his gross urges. Even instincts and emotions, the conservative feels, are on the whole more trustworthy guides than an unfettered reliance on his brain to guide him to the path of duty and away from the quest for unfettered power.

The welfare state destroys these resources as potent checks. Emotions and instincts become, not forces giving man the energy to discharge his duties, but reinforcements for his determination to do what he feels he has a right to do because he *wants* to do it. Social forces, too, cease to constrain him from following the path of least resistance, but rather conspire to help break down moral compunctions. Education will have already degenerated into the permissive kind. "Welfare" comes to mean, for both dispensers and recipients, the same as "wants." Standards have been eliminated. The sharpness and clearness of the head-on collision has been replaced by the mulish determination to ball through, come what may.

Every welfare state has been introduced by the wholesale trampling of traditions—which *have* grown naturally. The German Nazis under Hitler, the Russian Communists under Lenin, and the American New Dealers under Roosevelt have all sneered at the old ways of doing things. Religious, political, and economic traditions all come in for a drastic overhaul—or an attempt at drastic overhaul. Change in many cases seems to have been made for change's sake itself, with the newcomers to high places sometimes behaving like guilty youngsters climbing up to the cookie jar, who want to see how much they can get away with.

Struggle and Results vs. Power

A new factor thereupon emerges in the center of the liberal stage. We could call it "power" or we could call it "whim." In either case, it fills space where, for one reason or another, head-on collisions have ceased, and so are unable to generate results that are apparent to everyone. In the absence of authority established by these head-on collisions and results, an individual or group decrees authority by fiat. And by fiat that individual or group makes clear that it will promulgate the "welfare" for all the rest of us.

The builders of the power structure we know as the welfare state are what William James once called the "tender minded." They make such herculean efforts to avoid the head-on collision precisely because their minds are tender. The craving for power in the modern world is more a defensive wish to insulate oneself than it is an aggressive desire for aggrandizement. The theory of the welfare state, for instance, is precisely that men should be given what they need without a struggle. The ensuing softness and fuzziness will soon blur facts and dim reality. At the same time, power will constantly increase because nothing else is left: no real zest for life, no keen purposes, no gritting of teeth, no spirit of self-sacrifice, no will to win.

Checks and Balances vs. Power

Some governmental power is necessary. Our last line of defense against misuse of this power is to build checks and balances into government itself. We can separate the different levels of governments—local, state and national—in such a way as to make each, at least to some extent, suspicious and jealous of the others. We can separate government horizontally into executive, legislative, and judiciary, and divide the legislature into two houses. We can maintain two political parties of approximately equal strength, so there will always be an effective opposition. We can limit the powers delegated to government by the use of a written constitution.

Our liberal presidents did not deliberately seek personal power and personal aggrandizement. Perhaps not even Khrushchev or Hitler wanted all-power. But man is made to do the best he can in the conviction that he *is* right. He is made to fight with all he has, not to hold himself in. These men all thought themselves basically right. They had to think thus; otherwise they would have no confidence to get things done. And, like all men, sometimes they reacted without thinking at all. Sometimes they just didn't know what they did want. And sometimes they were spoiled.

But as long as they were met by checks and balances with nearly equal power moving in the other direction, things did not get too bad. The salvation of liberal presidents is that there *are* conservative congressmen, that there *is* a Republican Party, that they don't yet have omnipotent power over business and labor. But if the independent power of Congress, business, and the rest should vanish, the time of the mailed fist and the greased palm would already be here.

Power Welfare

Because the welfare state is not based on inner discipline, tradition, struggle and results, or checks and balances, it must be based on arbitrary power. And it is. In the first place, "welfare" means whatever those in authority say it means. In the second place, the men of welfare seem to become so very easily the men of power. And thirdly, the welfare state is its own judge of its own success.

We have seen that both the American New Deal and German National Socialism were welfare-state programs. A case could even be made out to show that the aim of George Orwell's sinister Insoc Party was a welfare state. Certainly that party was concerned that its members should be "goodthinkers," and spent a prodigiously large amount of time on this solicitude. The whole structure of Insoc was built on its control over definitions. "Freedom is Slavery," was one of the party slogans. "Happiness is Misery" or "Welfare is Ill-fare" would have been similarly appropriate. In Oceania, all loved Big Brother—and *that* was the real welfare. Or at least, since Big Brother had the power, who could say otherwise?

If one controlled the dictionary, "freedom" (to take a concept around which considerable controversy centers today) could be made to mean anything. So could "slavery." But once we perceive opposition between the two we are on our way toward a meaningful concept. It was precisely to abolish meanings that the Insoc system insisted on the equivalence of apparent contradictories. Our whole higher nature is based on antithesis—and it was the goal of the Insoc government to eliminate the higher nature of man. As such, it was the ultimate of welfare states. Appealing to the lower nature of man (which the liberal did not realize because he does not recognize a "lower nature of man"), it generated the power necessary to destroy man's higher nature. And it did so by perverting the very tools of reason that the liberals have taken such pains to perfect.

Leviathan Spits—

In the last decade or so, for the first time, the conservative is beginning to make his stand on the welfare state clear. Barry Goldwater and others tirelessly show the encroachment by the federal government in every field, saying, "The result is a Leviathan, a vast national authority out of touch with the people, and out of their control. This monolith of power is bounded only by the will of those who sit in high places." And they make it clear that this concentration of power could lead—in fact, is leading—to disaster.

While competition and conflict are indeed shrinking in extent, and under the liberals are no longer the general condition of man, they have become concentrated into the hard, tight conflict of the communist and the free world. And the more the opposing forces squeeze their power into centralization, the harder and tighter will this conflict become. The communist already has his welfare state—and the more the free world counters with our own version, the less will be the area of difference between communist and free man.

The liberal would of course rejoice at this narrowing of the gap, feeling that it would improve the chances of world peace. But instead it would dissipate them even further. For the great conflict that looms ahead is not a conflict of ideologies but a conflict of power. Two equally powerful slave states have less chance of living in peace with each other than if one were free—and much, much less than if both were.

—And the People Drown

The struggle over the welfare state will not become finally clear until the issue is seen to be, not the obligation of society to take care of its less fortunate members, but the concentration of power in the central government, that is, the destruction of individual responsibility. To observe how far the welfare state has strayed from its original humanitarian objectives, all one needs to do is to follow the veteran social worker on her rounds. Welfare today is a business—in some respects still softheaded, but in others more cold-blooded than any private corporation. Its most striking achievement has been not the alleviation of misery, but the transfer of authority and responsibility away from the individual, away from the family, away from local and state governments. And when this authority and responsibility is consolidated into the power of a vast impersonal welfare state, as George Orwell foresaw so well, that welfare state, looking for an outlet for its excess power, finds it in war.

CHAPTER EIGHT

Civil Rights and Human Wrongs

The liberals muffed their opportunity to bring about integration in the South by voluntary means. Now the question is: Can force bring integration, or will the bitter feeling being engendered between white and black wall the two races apart more than ever?

Real integration, either of peoples or of conflicting ideas, can be accomplished in only two ways: by a series of head-on collisions, which will teach each side respect for the other, or by the submergence of differences in an overriding purpose. Liberalism seems calculated almost expressly to nullify both possibilities.

The One-Party South and Integration

After the War Between the States, the Democratic Party secured a stranglehold on the South. For a hundred years this strangling monopoly prevented the type of head-on collision that elsewhere in the nation was bringing "irreconcilable" points of view together. In every northern and western election, one side or the other (or both) would give a little or take a little. If the two-party system had prevailed in the South during these hundred years, the feeling there between white and Negro would probably be much the same as it is in those northern cities where the Negro population is large.

With an active two-party political system it would have been inconceivable that the potential political power of the southern Negro, who represents more than one third of the population in some of the southern states, would have been ignored. One party or the other, at least during hotly fought elections, would have been sure to appeal for Negro votes—and with political interest in Negro votes, the tight cords of segregation would inevitably have been loosened. As it happened, however, political stagnation set in and enabled the segregationists to hang on to outworn ideas, which probably not even they were thoroughly convinced of any more, but which they hung on to even more stubbornly for that very reason. And the longer the South swung segregation by its tail, the harder it was to let go.

Liberalism cannot be blamed for the whole century of segregation. But the famous Roosevelt coalition of minorities, which kept the southern segregationists and the Negroes in the same party, smothered the first real chance the southern Negro had.

When, in the thirties, southern cities started growing, the South itself began to recognize the burden both of its one-party system and of at least certain aspects of segregation. But by that time the liberal administration in Washington, needing southern electoral votes, gave every encouragement in its power to the South's one-party system, partly to make up for the unpalatability of its economic policies. And the one-party system had become inextricably intertwined with extreme segregationism.

During the very years when the southern economic and social structure was changing, to make possible a New Deal in the South, the New Deal in Washington and its successors kept sweeping the problem under the rug. Perhaps it was not deliberate, but the effect was the same as if it had been—keeping the South under the thumb of the Democratic machine, and so maintaining segregation.

In this way, the liberals are to blame for the outbreaks of racial violence in the South.

The Answer Is Duty

Besides the head-on collision, the other method of achieving integration is to bury the obsession for rights into a concern for duty. Abraham Lincoln thought of the relationship between man and man more as being regulated by the centripetal concept of "duty" than by the centrifugal concept of "rights." The Great Emancipator did not free the slaves to protect their civil rights. Morally, his concern was more with the degradation of the white race resulting from the ownership of man by man. The Civil War, in modern terminology, was fought for duties rather than rights.

The real meaning of the war, however, was lost in Reconstruction days. The war itself would not have proved an insurmountable barrier to the integration of North and South. But Reconstruction was just plain force. The southern white started brooding about his "rights"—and segregation was the result.

Today, of course, it is the Negro, not the southern white, who is so vociferously demanding his "rights." The two cases differ in that the whites have been the group in power. But the Negro's demand for freedom of access to educational facilities, lunch counters, toilets, and so on, has many earmarks of similarity with the segregationist's demand for "freedom of association."

The problem produced by these two conflicting sets of "rights" is insoluble except by force—which is no solution. It can be resolved only by restating the whole problem. Instead of the question: Who has the stronger rights? it should be: Where does one's duty to his country, his home, his God, lie?

This second question may be a very complex one or a very simple one, but it is one to which an answer, especially with the help of a series of head-on collisions, can be made because the concept of duty already contains the concept of "rights."

Indeed, during conservative periods of history, "rights" and "duties" are reverse sides of the same coin. Even today some dictionary definitions of "right" and "duty" are hardly distinguishable. Webster notes that the "earliest ascertainable" meaning of "right" is "That which is right or correct; . . . adherence to duty; *a.* obedience to lawful authority; freedom from guilt; . . . that which is warranted by moral approval, the ideal of moral propriety; *b.* Just or righteous action or decision; justice; as, to petition as a matter of right."

"Right" is an Anglo-Saxon word that originally included the *concept* of duty; as the word "duty" penetrated the English language from the French (and as liberalism began corrupting the traditional meaning of words), "right" lost any connotation of duty, and became restricted to "claim" or "prerogative." But the closeness of the original association between "right" and "duty" can be seen by comparing Webster's definition of "right," as above, with the following Funk and Wagnalls' definition of "duty": "the obligation to do that which is required, especially by the moral law; moral obligation; right action."

Racial violence in the South as well as possibly all of our modern problems of extremism can be traced to such idea-splitting as that of the kind that took "duty" out of "right." Racial violence—and the other types of violence in the modern world—can usually be traced back to the liberal's passion for "rights" and other values that are centrifugal in nature. The only answer to violence (and coercion) that the authors know of is acceptance of the centripetal principle of duty. But it is doubtful whether modern liberals have ever been able to comprehend the meaning of that concept.

Certainly, if they do, they give little evidence of it. As the summer of 1964 approached it became obvious that the Negro extremists believed they had a "right" to wreck the New York World's Fair—or do anything else that occurred to them. Where did they get that idea? Why, from the only place they could: from the incessant preaching of the liberals about "rights" unfettered by "duties."

The Liberal's Resounding Whisper to Duty

At present, it takes a very acute sense of hearing to catch any signs of a liberal recognition that there *is* such a thing as "duty." It was not always thus. A report to the American Economic Association, some years ago, stated: "We hold that the doctrine of *laissez faire* is unsafe in politics and unsound in morals. . . . All have duties as well as rights, and, as Emerson said several years ago, it is time we heard more about duties and less about rights."

But with their victory over what they were (and still are) pleased to call *laissez faire,* the liberals' interest in duties seems to have evaporated. Instead, they spend their energies trying to establish the right of Negroes to attend the same schools whites do; the right of teachers to defy orders of the legislators and even of their own administrative superiors; the right of soldiers to escape discipline; the rights of all young people to attend college; the right of old people to have free medicare; the right of writers to write whatever they want and readers to read whatever they choose, no matter how pornographic; the right of homosexuals to practice their persuasion; the right of suspected communists and fellow travelers to be immune from "persecution"; the right of hardened criminals to escape capital punishment; the right of romantically inclined (but not wedded) couples to be furnished with birth control information and aids; the right of labor unions to require all employees of a given company to join the union; the right of the government to spend more than it takes in; the right of mothers to receive aid-for-dependent-children allotments for their illegitimate offspring (and at the same time "see" the fathers); the right of colonial nations to be independent; the right of underdeveloped nations to economic development; the right of everyone to be happy.

It is not the job of the conservative to take up cudgels against these rights any more than it is to fight for them. There is, for example, no conservative principle for segregation any more than for integration. If the Negro really wants integration, the conservative can only wish him Godspeed in head-on collision to win it, and at the same time make sure that the struggle does not mortally injure society. The only rights the conservative is called upon to defend are the basic right of self-determination of all free peoples, which rests on property rights; the right of the individual to whatever privacy is not in conflict with his responsibilities, and the right to use his own initiative. Beyond that the conservative's mission lies, not with extending the area of "civil rights," but with that concept the liberal so resoundingly neglects, which Blackstone calls "civil duties."

The Right of Initiative

While the liberal is concentrating so hard on proving that people have the right of taking in, the conservative tries to save as much as possible of the right of putting out. In the past, the right of a man to give forth whatever energies he had within himself to give—that is, initiative and enterprise—was not considered a "right," but more like a duty or a responsibility. But now that red tape, regimentation, orders from on high, and punitive taxation are strangling initiative, it is coming to be recognized as one of the most precious rights we have.

In the field of the arts and sciences, the thing we know in business as initiative and free enterprise, is called creativity. We know very little about creativity. We know little more about what makes a man a self-starter, even though we do know a great deal about ways and means of unmaking him.

And we do know that the reason America became strong was the enterprise of millions of her citizens. Her resources, her spaciousness, her climate and geography, her melting-pot characteristics—all were factors, but without adventurous people willing and able to try new things, take risks, and bear the consequences, the America we know simply would not have been built.

The liberal should be aware of this as well or better than the conservative. For the virtues of initiative and enterprise were originally largely liberal virtues. But modern liberalism has become corrupt, and in the place of individual initiative it tries to substitute something it calls "economic planning," designed to accomplish through arm-chair reasoning the same things that the builders of our country and its economy accomplished through struggle, risk, sacrifice, work, guts, inspiration, drive, and just plain luck. Under economic planning, initiative would cease to be either a right or a duty.

The liberal seems to be trying to drive out all signs of individual enterprise except the kind that conforms to welfare state edicts, which is, of course, a contradiction in terms. Society itself is the interweaving of strands of individual enterprise. When the welfare state has made society both stagnant and unnecessary, private enterprise will also become unnecessary.

Man's Oldest Right

Senator Goldwater once observed that property was man's most sacred right. It is also man's oldest right. Property rights go back not only to the earliest days of antiquity, but millions and millions of years before man even became man. As we have already noted, for wild animals the drive to hold property is even stronger than that of sex.

During the days when liberalism was forming its dogmas, the biological roots of the drive to acquire property were not remotely suspected. As a consequence, liberals put a low value on property rights and a high one on what they call "human rights." Not until the British ornithologist Eliot Howard showed that male birds fight over real-estate holdings rather than over females did the truth begin to come out. Max Eastman describes Howard's findings: "Male birds of migrant species," he writes, "fly north ahead of the females, and each stakes out a piece of territory which shall belong to him. He stakes it out with song, and defends its boundaries with belligerent ardor. Then the females arrive; and if his holdings are secure, he has small trouble getting a discriminating bride to join him. The fighting over her is negligible.

"Birds post their property by singing, but most mammals, since they live in a world of smells rather than sounds, do it by 'demarcating,' which means depositing a characteristic scent at the boundaries of their domain. Lions and tigers perform this function with their urine. Other animals have a special gland designed for this sole purpose. Among some deer and antelope, a gland above the eye produces a strong-smelling oily substance which, rubbed off on twigs and branches, impregnates the whole dwelling place with a notice of ownership."

Man is the only mammal known to deny property rights. When he does, the confusion and frustration produced by the repression of an instinct that nature has provided erupts in the twisted, distorted grimaces of communism.

The term "private property" derives from two Latin words, one meaning "one's own" or "proper," and the other meaning "apart from the state." Literally, "private property" therefore indicates a characteristic of the individual that he refuses to share with the state, such as his relationship with family and friends. In prying this concept loose from its moorings, the liberals are inflicting on millions the sense of being lost in a meaningless world.

The liberals utterly lack comprehension of the meaning of property. They reveal this defect when they use the terms "property rights" and "human rights" as antithetical. Actually, property rights are simply a device of individual responsibility by which an individual may partake of some of the scarce riches of the world without feeling that he is beholden to anybody. Property rights are both the basis for democracy and the counterbalance to political power. Without them, the politicians would have to settle all questions. For this and for other reasons, property rights are the chiefest of the human rights.

The Responsibility of Rights

In order for a right to be a real right (rather than simply power), it *must* be responsible, earned. Otherwise, at best, it is only a bit of welfare, a gift from a benevolent police state. Such a right would subtract from individual dignity, rather than add to it. Rights are God-given, and should not be tampered with by a bureaucrat or even Congress. Not even the Constitutional fathers presumed to "grant" rights. All they did was to set up the machinery whereby men could prove themselves.

Children have few rights. Why? Because they are irresponsible; that is, they are not men (and women). Criminals and the insane lack rights for the same reason. The only justification that, in a democracy, gives the color of validity to unwillingness to permit the Negro to exercise the same rights as the white man is the suspicion that Negroes are not capable of full responsibility. When they demonstrate they are, nothing save a dictator can keep them from earning the same acceptance that Jews, Irishmen, Italians, Poles, and others who have had to fight discrimination have won.

Mr. Meredith and "Ole Miss"

In addition to the sin of omission, in discouraging the South from the two-party head-on collisions that would have brought about normal race relations in that section, the liberal is guilty of a sin of commission in encouraging irresponsibility. The case of James Meredith illustrates this.

In 1962, Meredith, a Negro, applied for admission to the University of Mississippi, which had never knowingly enrolled a Negro student. Ole Miss refused his application, saying he was not qualified. The federal government contended he had a constitutional right to enter, and insisted that he be enrolled. He was—after Washington had sent in soldiers and federal marshals, and after a pitched battle that destroyed much of the town of Oxford, had injured many, and left two men dead. After Meredith was accepted, some of the soldiery left. Others dug in for a long encampment. Escorted to and from classes by his federal guardians, and generally treated with stony silence by his classmates, Meredith apparently became so unhappy he couldn't study. At the end of the first semester, he was failing in most of his subjects, and barely passing in the others. He wanted to drop out.

For what was now Meredith's purpose? Originally he was a single-minded and dedicated man. He wanted to break into Ole Miss and prove that a colored student could do as well or better than the white ones. He would then become a hero to his people and would have laid another milestone in the history of race relations in the South.

But all this was dependent on his ability to stand up and do things by himself. If he failed, or even if he succeeded only because of being propped up by the government, his whole dream would turn to dust and ashes. And that is precisely what governmental intervention did to James Meredith the man. From being the star of the play, Meredith rapidly became a pawn to be moved around as the winds of politics blew. He was not happy, he was not making progress in his studies, he realized he was losing precious time out of his own life and not making any appreciable contributions to his people. He couldn't even be sure that, if his grades were to improve, the improvement would be due to his own efforts and ability or to government pressure. He must have frequently been troubled by a sickly feeling that perhaps he was only making things worse. He was trapped.

Freedmen and Freemen

If the federals had not intervened, of course, there is little likelihood that Meredith would have been admitted to Ole Miss at that particular time. The argument of the liberals is clear, for once: federal intervention is necessary to bring integration to the South in the lifetimes of those now living. Conceivably, through a series of head-on collisions in which he had to rely on his own resources, it would take the Negro, who in 1963 had been a slave a hundred years before, another century to fully establish his right to freedom in equality with the white man—whose ancestors had begun their struggle for freedom and civilization thousands of years ago. A century, Negroes and liberals said, is too long to wait.

But *this is the only way*. What the Negro hopes to become he must become by himself. That has been the way for all men in the past, and it will always be the way as long as men are men. People—or the welfare state—can give you things, but those things inevitably turn out to be different from the things you earned yourself. To the extent that Uncle Sam takes the Negro race by the hand and nursemaids it along, it will fail to acquire responsibility.

The white man committed a great crime in making slaves of the Negro. By the War Between the States and Reconstruction, he punished himself. In the process, the Negroes were freed; that is, the legal handicaps to freedom were removed. But the Negro was not yet a free man. No, he had to forge that for himself. And in millions of Negro homes after 1865 he did begin this process of learning responsibility, self-discipline, initiative—and so becoming morally free. Some say he had accomplished his goal by the 1960s, or even long before. Others say that he needs to improve himself more before he is fit for togetherness and that, by and large, he is still a different breed. This argument can only be settled by a head-on collision in which Negroes stand up to their critics without the help of federal bayonets. They face a formidable task? Assuredly. But they would not be the first to win out in the face of odds. All human progress, in fact, has been a history of just such head-on collisions against odds.

The Head-on Collision vs. Welfare Rights

The close link between the liberal's advocacy of "civil rights" for the Negro and his advocacy of welfare for the old, the young, the dependent, the unemployed, the farmer, the sick, the under-developed, seems to have escaped comment. Yet the underlying philosophy is exactly the same. "These people deserve things," the liberal says, "so let the government give them to them."

The conservative does not dispute that the people are deserving. Instead, he suggests that instead of "rights" being in question, the issue is whether or not a Design is being upset by welfare-state handouts. The conservative isn't willing to take for granted that those things a man wants, or that will make him most comfortable and give him the greatest sense of security, are necessarily the things he should have. The Divine Plan seems to call for suffering and pain. It could even be, the conservative may muse, that the financial stringencies caused by unemployment and sickness have a lesson to teach a man—or that when we smother necessity with kindness, we are keeping that of which she might become the mother from ever being born.

In the days before welfare rights, life was a constant series of head-on collisions between the individual and his environment. Whatever the precise nature of the head-on collision, it always brought with it a strong gust of reality. Men might suffer temporarily, but they always knew where they were. And the head-on collisions brought experience and learning. They made it necessary for the individual to take initiative. They required him to assume responsibility for himself and his loved ones. They forced him to balance the risks of different uncertainties against each other and against the stagnation of a state of comparative risklessness. They kept together the two sides of the coin: give and receive, outgo and income, duty and rights. They infused him with a deep sense of purpose.

Now come welfare rights. They blunt all this. Under the welfare state the necessities of life are handed around to all comers, at least to all who abstain from rocking the boat. Even the right to happiness is considered something to be given out by the state, rather than earned. The goal of the welfare state is not simply welfare rights for the poor and weak. Its goal is welfare—and the rights this implies—for all, even if to achieve it means that all must become poor and weak. Let's look, for instance, at medicare.

The Right to Hypochondria

Medicare may well help to *undermine* national health. The liberal's medicare plea assumes basically that health is something relatively simple that can be objectively determined, and that we know what it is. These assumptions may be wrong. Both ill health and recovery from ill health may be tremendously more complicated than the liberal has any notion of.

Liberals assume that a "bug," *or* a chemical imbalance, *or* a malfunctioning, *or* a structural defect is the cause of disease. Medicine seems to be moving in the direction of finding that these "causes" do not operate singly, but that two or more have to cooperate. It may be that physicians of the future will regard all of these factors more as symptoms than as causes.

Many if not most doctors today will agree that most sickness is psychosomatic in origin. While applying that label does not "solve" anything, it does push the cause of ill health back and back and back—perhaps even back into mysteries as deep as Christianity itself.

In his *Will to Live,* Dr. Arnold Hutschnecker points out that, in a sense, many if not most sick people may *want* to be sick. Since people who "want" their ill health may suffer severely from it, it is obvious that the operation of this mechanism must be extremely devious. It would certainly be devious enough that the mere availability of "free" medical care wouldn't cure it.

But "free" medicare could well make it worse. Cases in which the psychosomatic origin of ill health seems most definitely established tend to have certain characteristics in common. The patient shows an inability to accept life. He seems to keep expecting—and expecting with too great an intensity—things that are just not in the cards. At the same time, he expects them to come to him without real effort or sacrifices on his part. In his mind, there has been a split between his rights and his duties. Psychosomatic victims may be suffering from a severe case of irresponsibility.

If so, the best tonic the patient could have would be to pay, in some open and aboveboard manner, for what he is asking from life. A good way to start would be to pay the doctor. There is nothing like paying bills to bring a cooling air of reality.

On the other hand, to give everyone the right to "see" a doctor free whenever he thinks something is wrong with him is a good deal like paying people to get sick.

Power From Health

Medicare may be diametrically the wrong way to go about improving the health of the people. But it is the right way to go about centralizing power in Washington. As Walter Reuther told the House Committee on Ways and Means in July 1959, when the Forand Bill was the white hope of the medicare enthusiasts: "Even if we were against national health insurance, we would favor passage of the Forand Bill." The transformation of the aged (to be followed by other groups) into wards of a state that would have access to all formerly confidential records between patient and physician would go far toward ushering in the age of Big Brother. Besides, the bringing to heel of the entire medical profession would be no mean achievement in itself.

And when the government finally got its fingers into mental health, Big Brother would be really ready to set up operations. Illiberal sentiments and mental aberrations would become synonymous, not because the liberals were deliberately trying to "get" their enemies, but because obviously those who are not liberals must be either ignorant or cracked. The 1962 decision of a New York City judge who committed a slum apartment owner to a mental hospital shows what is likely to happen. Explained the judge in that case: "I think you are a cruel, vicious man, and I don't think you could possibly be normal."

Rights of Murderers

On the other hand, there have been quite a number of cases in which probably insane criminals have been executed. The rights of the criminally insane may have been trampled in these cases. California's Governor Edmund Brown, a good liberal, appointed a Commission on Insanity and Criminal Offenders largely because of his shock and chagrin at such executions as that of Stephen Nash, shaggy-haired and toothless killer who had laughingly boasted he had killed ten men and a boy for the satisfaction it gave him. This, Governor Brown knew, was almost prima facie evidence that Nash had been insane. And yet the courts had gone ahead and ordered his execution!

In an effort to introduce more respect for the rights of murderers, the report of the governor's commission proposed that the law on insanity be changed. At present, under the M'Naghten Rule, the only two insanity defenses are if the accused did not "know the nature and quality of the act he was doing, or if he did know it, that he did not know that what he was doing was wrong." The Brown Commission felt the law should read instead:

"A person is not criminally responsible for an act if, at the time of his commission of such act, as a substantial consequence of a mental disorder, he did not have the adequate capacity to conform his conduct to the requirements of the law he is alleged to have violated." The Commission explained that "mental disorder" referred "not only to mental illness and disease but also to mental defects, which would include offenders of inferior intelligence." Jack Goulding suggests that "it is not inconceivable that this definition could also include moral depravity." The more morally depraved a criminal is, the less likely that he would be punished, under the liberal ruling.

Right vs. Right

On all "rights" problems, the conservatives and liberals have a different point of view. Regardless of whether the administration in power in Washington is Republican or Democratic, the conservatives, in most cases, would put states' rights ahead of Negro integration; the right of taxpayers to spend their own money ahead of the rights of foreign nations, farmers, federal education interests, and similar claimants to share it; the right of society to public safety ahead of the right of the criminally insane to life, liberty and the pursuit of happiness; the right of a community to prescribe standards for the literature likely to reach its members, and especially its youth, ahead of the right of writers to write whatever kind of book they want to, the right of publishers to publish it, the right of booksellers to distribute it, or the right of individuals to read it; the right of a privately owned company ahead of the right of one owned by the federal government; the right of privacy ahead of the rights of intellectual or even "scientific" curiosity, the right of Christian parents to have their children grow up with religious beliefs and moral standards over the right of atheists to shut out all thought of anything they don't understand. Liberals prefer the reverse side of these controversies—although they would, of course, phrase them differently. For that matter, the conservative also should rephrase them. The conservative now talks in terms of "rights" only because he is habituated to liberal terminology. For the conservative to be concerned about "rights" as such, in the current meaning of that word, is almost a contradiction in terms. It is for the liberal to worry about "rights." The conservative, to the extent that he *is* a conservative, thinks in terms of the combined package of rights-plus-duties. And rights-plus-duties equal responsibility.

The problem, as the conservative sees it, is to determine which one of a multitude of competing responsibilities should prevail under given circumstances. And, in the view of the conservative, this should be as little as possible a question for government to determine. The problem—or rather the challenge—is for the individual to decide of his own free will where his primary responsibility lies. But as we have suggested before "free will" doesn't mean "free" in the liberal sense of escaping responsibility. If a man decides wrong, he will find himself being punished in one way or another—possibly even to the point where he becomes less of a man and less of an individual. This is, for the conservative, what "responsibility" means.

PART THREE

Perspectives

CHAPTER NINE

The Liberal Mystique

The liberal mystique almost defies definition because our very words nowadays are loaded with liberal mysticism. The liberal believes the world owes him a living. He believes he can eat his cake and have it too. He believes that actions and motives can be adequately described in words. He believes that by spending money we really save it. He believes in making agreements with communist countries, even though he doesn't trust them to keep agreements. He believes that man, who is made to fight for what he wants and for what he believes is right, can be impartial and "neutralist." He believes nonmilitary men are usually better judges of military requirements than military men. There is in fact no end to these mystical beliefs of the liberal.

All of them, we might add, result from his denying the mainstem of conservative belief, that man is utterly dependent on God, from which springs the entire philosophy of conservatism.

This liberal mystique surrounds reality with a dense haze. And since it is even more necessary to women than to men to always carry inside them a feeling of reality, women are the chief sufferers from the liberal mystique.

The Liberal Mystique and the Head-on Collision

In the liberal mystique, the head-on collision becomes all but impossible. Both men and women are really creatures of the head-on collision, but men can, perhaps at great cost, postpone it almost indefinitely. Women can't. The very biological function of a woman is based on a head-on collision occurring within her body that will give birth to new life. Women, even more than men, can be happy, and know they are happy, only in the presence of continual but well-spaced, man-sized head-on collisions, that alone can give a sense of reality.

Neither the liberal mystique nor any other mystique, however, can survive the head-on collision. This is, we think, why conservatism usually follows war—although liberalism may precede it. Even the head-on collision of meeting a payroll, or of balancing a budget, leads to conservatism. Any sharp, clear-cut struggle or opposition cuts through the liberal mystique and dissipates it, partly because it focuses attention and effort away from theory and onto practice. Every debate, even, helps to blow away the liberal mystique, because, while a debate does consist of theory and words, it requires rigorous use of both, it emphasizes exact facts, and, most importantly, it makes each debating team try to win, not by mouthing abstractions, but by *convincing the judges.*

Liberal vs. Woman

The practical effect of the liberal mystique, as far as a woman is concerned, is to force her to live in what we can call to start with "a man's world." Her children are put through a school system devised by and run by men. The teachers, and even the principal, in the lower grades may be women, but they are supposed only to carry out the instructions of the large-domed men who decided that the mission of education is to cater to the "needs and tensions of youth." Two-thirds of the married women are set up to keep house for a lordly male, a parcel of children, and possibly an in-law of his or hers. "Keeping house" usually means mainly getting meals on time, meeting male-inspired deadlines, using mechanical appliances devised by men, and seeking to make the man of the house comfortable and happy. One third of the wives work—which probably means that they have a second male boss to please, even more appliances to run and pamper, and new schedules to keep.

The liberal has never taken full cognizance of the difference between male and female. Just as he regards the conservative as a second-rate liberal, so, in most situations, he regards woman as a second-rate man. To be sure, the liberal will protest this libel on him, but the authors have talked to too many liberals not to know that this is so.

Liberals prate about "equal rights," but they are the first ones to protest a diminution in male prerogatives. In business, it is almost an axiom that the more liberal a man is (or thinks he is), the more he resents having a woman supervisor, and the more arguments he is able to think of why women should be kept in their clerical "place" as stenographers, filing clerks, assemblers of small parts, and so on, while the men monopolize the professional and managerial jobs.

The vote in the House of Representatives on the Smith Amendment to the Civil Rights Bill of 1964 makes this clear. Congressman Howard Smith of Virginia suggested that the bill contain a phrase prohibiting discrimination against women as well as against Negroes. In order to fall in with his suggestions, only two words—"and sex"—would have to be added to the clause outlawing "race, color, religion, or national origin" as grounds for discrimination by employers and labor unions. Almost all the liberal northern Democrats voted against the Smith piece of "illogic." The conservative Democrats and Republicans, however, put it over, 168 to 133.

Man of Words vs. Man of Action

The liberal is primarily a man of words. The conservative is primarily a man of action. In a sense, this difference between liberal and conservative is the most fundamental of all their differences, and the one to which all the others can be traced.

Insufficient understanding of this basic fact, we think, is the reason liberals and conservatives, as well as legitimately disagreeing, misunderstand and misconstrue each other. Such misunderstanding sometimes reaches the ludicrous, as when the liberal, proposing the same remedies that the Gracchi tried in ancient Rome, calls the conservative a "reactionary" for not endorsing them.

As the "man of words," the liberal feels that anything that can be put down in logical fashion in, say, a textbook, can be duplicated in fact—and, conversely, that any fact or action can be adequately summed up in words. These beliefs, which the conservative knows to be fallacious, are at the bottom of most, if not all, of the liberal's troubles. The liberal's theories of coexistence, the welfare state, economic planning, *et al.*, sound so good when put down in words—*but they just don't work out,* at least under the conditions of the twentieth century.

The conservative, as the man of action, thinks of words, not in their logical meaning so much as in the light of their purpose as an adjunct to action, to motives, and to the development of fact. Elton Mayo expressed the conservative point of view perfectly when he said, "I no longer try to think what men mean by what they say; I try to think why they say it." To the conservative, words are very definitely only a tool; to the liberal, words are almost the be-all and end-all of life.

The conservative knows that words are more likely than action to bring unhappiness rather than happiness. Action, on the other hand, may bring tragedy. It may be evil. But action cannot be "bad" in the sense a word—or an *in*action—can be. Women especially are the victims of the frenzied desire on the part of their liberal menfolk to substitute words (and inaction) for action. Probably, indeed, most disagreements between men and women stem from the man's reverence for the word as relatively independent of either things or action, and the woman's unwillingness to play *that* game. (Here the authors are, of course, only attempting to restate the age-old argument between man's "reason" and woman's "intuition.")

Theory on the Rocks

Considering the liberals' worship of words and their belief in the omnipotence of what words can build, one can only feel sorry for them after witnessing the downfall of one after another of their wordy programs, which started out with such a flourish.

Take the farm program as an example. It sounded so simple and so utterly "right" for the government, which at the time of World War I and World War II brought on so much of the farmer's troubles by encouraging an expansion of production, to guarantee "parity" prices in an effort to jack him back up to where he should be. There is no question but that the farmer was getting the short end of the deal, with soaring production combining with an only moderately growing market to send farm prices down—especially as the prices for the industrial products he bought tended to be "sticky" and often remained high in spite of market conditions that should have theoretically pulled them down too.

If the farm question could be narrowed down to the issue of whether or not the farmers "deserved" a new deal, there would be little argument against a governmentally run farm program. But it can't. The basic question, we began to realize after thirty years, was: Can the government do anything about it except to make things worse?

In 1933 and 1934, such a question would have seemed silly,

at least to the eager New Dealers who believed the government could do anything—as silly as the similar question whether the United States Government could really help the underdeveloped nations by pouring in foreign aid would have seemed, in the early 1960s, to the more tired but still game New Frontiersmen. But after thirty years and billions of dollars spent on the farm program, with the problem at the end bigger than ever (and after $100 billion of foreign aid, with the problem *that* was designed to alleviate bigger than ever), there is room for the suspicion that the answer all along has been no.

By the 1960s, almost all the liberal programs seemed to be turning out the same way. The government kept pouring in money, both domestically and internationally, and the problems got worse and worse. Not only the farm program and foreign aid, but all welfare and "emergency" measures of one kind or another, instead of shrinking grew and grew and grew.

Even by early 1964, indeed, many were beginning to feel sorry for President Johnson. His domestic program had seemed to work out well for Franklin Delano Roosevelt. Why, oh, why, didn't it work for Lyndon Baines Johnson? On paper it looked much the same.

And in the foreign field, at least where the vagaries of the liberal mind permitted, the Johnson moves followed the best orthodox liberal doctrines to the fullest extent it was politically "safe" to do so: coexistence, consultation, communication, cooperation, disengagement, neutrality, objectivity, and so on. But they didn't work out. Why? Why? Why?

It is high time to assess whether there may be limits to liberalism—not only whether or not there may be limits to what the United States Government, or even a world government, may be able to accomplish, but whether indeed it is possible to "solve" any "problem" of this nature by reducing it to words, and then trying to put those words into action. Can the world be swung by words?

The Mystique Symbols

The conservative feels that life—the power to "make things happen"—has been given him for a very definite purpose; the liberal is not likely to believe very profoundly in any final ends or purposes, but contends that, since he does find himself here, he had better make the best of it, that is, do good deeds, be comfortable, get pleasure, be happy. The liberal concentrates on means, not ends—and these means usually take the shape of, or are related to, words and other symbols.

To be sure, there may well be "purposes" for the liberal, but these purposes are attenuated, dispersed, nebulous. They, like all the rest of liberalism, are abstractions. The whole life of the modern liberal is a life of symbol; it never gets down to reality.

For thirty years and more, the liberal has waged bitter war against the "economic royalist" and the "imperialist." But the honest liberal would be the first to admit that, at least in late twentieth-century America, there *are* no economic royalists nor imperialists. The liberals denounce symbols and conditions rather than men. "Communist" is a symbol to the liberal rather than a depraved man, as the conservative interprets it. "Negro" to the liberal is a symbol of someone discriminated against, not a man who is mixed good and evil like all other men.

In his warfare against "imperialism," the liberal seems to have only thought that ex-colonies would simply become "free" (again merely a symbol to the modern liberal), neither recognizing the ambitions and passions of men nor showing any awareness that the "colonials" were often really only savages. For the most part, the liberal now refuses to believe that, because of his inability to see the reality for the symbol, Africa is now a vast area of declining standards of living and rising lawlessness where Catholic priests and nuns are butchered, and where whole tribes of superior people, such as the Watusi, are tortured and thrown, bound, into the river to drown. The liberal, with eyes only for symbols, refuses to believe even United Nations evidence that the Diem government in South Vietnam, which he labeled "fascist," was not wantonly oppressing the Buddhists. There are still liberals who believe that the troika system in Laos could have worked, that Castro is merely an agrarian reformer, and that the United States, to rid itself of the devastating name "imperialist," must renounce the Panama Canal.

There may, in the history of the world, never have been a more virulent disease, nor one harder to treat, than this mystique of the liberals, which seems indeed to be carried on the night air.

Instead of "night air," however, it would be more correct to say the liberal mystique is borne by impenetrable symbols. All around the liberal there is nothing but symbols. He has drained life itself of its satisfying juices, and, with Bertrand Russell, confesses he would rather be red than dead. Deprived of a central vitality—of purpose that is more than a symbol—the symbols themselves of liberalism are becoming hopelessly tangled and confused one with another.

If such a metaphor be permitted, the liberal symbols—for freedom, for democracy, for the good life—can perhaps best be described as having become knotted. Legend has it that Alexander the Great was once faced with just such a tangle. The yoke and axletree of the wagon of Gordius, king of the Phrygians, were fastened by the intricate Gordian knot, which defied all efforts to untie. Rumor spread that he who undid the Gordian knot would be ruler of all Asia. When Alexander was shown it, he raised his sword and severed it with a stroke. The knot vanished.

CHAPTER TEN

The Challenge of Conservatism

At least since 1945 we have been living in a new world. Perhaps the change taking place in the twentieth century is as profound as that of the fourteenth and fifteenth centuries. Perhaps we are entering a new Renaissance.

The new world is not of conservative making any more than the original Renaissance was. But the conservative may be the only one who can deal with it. Indeed this possibility is coming to appear more and more probable. The question is becoming, not whether the conservative *will* take over or *can* take over, but will he take over *in time?*

Resurgent Conservatism

Young people are talking conservatism. "Conservatism" has, in the last few years, become a household term. Polls of public opinion show startling conservative gains. Books on conservatism coming off the presses in a steady stream become best sellers. Articles on conservatism are starting to appear in magazines and periodicals of all kinds. Lectures, speeches, newscasts, TV plays, are featuring this "new" and fascinating idea. Liberals are being thrown back on the defensive for the first time in a generation.

But it is not the renewed interest in and allegiance to the name "conservatism" that is, for the conservative, the most heartening thing. Even more encouraging is the effort in everyday life by which we are trying to claw our way back to the principles of conservatism, whether we know it or not.

In the face of the world-wide communist threat to the basis of morality, and the apparent moral decline in many parts of the Western world, the United States is witnessing a revulsion against immorality. Immorality in the United States continues and is probably increasing, but the growing distaste for it even by men of the world is even more striking. Since conservatives contend that society is built on morality and principle, while the liberals say it is built on reason, increasing preoccupation with moral problems is a sign of conservative revival.

The revolt against the liberal philosophy of the welfare state is coming in most unexpected ways. For instance, the defense industry, which to a degree has been the recipient of government "welfare" since the outbreak of World War II, is in revolt against the resulting inefficiency. To select only a small illustration, when procedures analysts, whose job it is to see that their companies do things in the most efficient way, talk among themselves, the conversation usually comes around to the impossibility of making an operation efficient when its very basis derives from welfare-type thinking on the part of the government. Although procedures analysts seldom use the word "corruption," they seem to agree that the fundamental problem they are struggling with is indeed corruption resulting from relations between government and industry based on loose (and at the same time dogmatic) liberal thinking.

As a generalization, it can be said that modern corruption is more likely to arise from looseness than from out-and-out rascality. In this sense there is a close family resemblance between the Billie Sol Estes and Bobby Baker conniving, the "TFX-type" confusion, the flagrant Chicago destruction of Nixon ballots in 1960, and welfare handouts to everyone who can establish a "need."

The revolt among the smaller cogs in the defense industry against liberalism, however, is not limited to disgust over inefficiency and corruption. Contract people, engineers, proposal writers, are increasingly incensed by the Pentagon's effort to eliminate (or at least to pretend to eliminate) the human equation. Secretary McNamara and his boys are wildly enthusiastic about computers.

But it is beginning to dawn on the defense industry that sometimes all computers do is to give the appearance of efficiency to something that is basically inefficient, and even perhaps basically corrupt. Obviously, business relations should try to avoid "personalities," but the conservative way is to accept the necessary elements of personality and build safeguards while the liberal way is to determinedly overlook the fact that even relationships in business are basically personal relations. In this way, incidentally, the liberal computerizes "welfare."

All through America human nature is crying out against the application of liberal doctrines. One example is the opposition of all kinds of people to profligate spending practices, especially foreign aid. Another is the stiffening opposition to favoritism to labor or the Negro. Parents are up in arms against the determination of such liberal-dominated organizations as the National Education Association in persisting in educational practices, such as the sight method of teaching reading as opposed to phonetics, the only method that has ever taught Johnny to read. A grassroots protest against the Supreme Court's attempt to ban religion in the schools is gaining momentum. People are waking up, looking at each other dizzily and asking each other: "How long have we been asleep and dreaming?"

The Conservative Side

Just what is the main point on which the conservative is challenging? Unlike the liberal, the conservative is not too much concerned about ideologies as such. What he says today, in a voice that is becoming increasingly loud and clear, is that we are failing in our governmental approach—and must cut loose and try a different one before it is too late.

Specifically, the conservative wants to repair the breach between words and action. He wants to do this by making words again the handmaiden of action, instead of vice versa, and so free us from our paralysis where all we seem able to do is to talk and talk and talk but not act.

On Cuba, the conservative says, "Quit just talking and *do* something—slap on a blockade, encourage hit-and-run forays by the Cuban exiles, maintain a force of anti-Castro guerrillas in the Cuban hills and mountains, infiltrate Castro's forces, undermine his support, devise a more appealing program than his for the Cuban people and sell it to them over his head. But *do* something."

On fiscal policy, the conservative says: "Quit just spending and spending like a drunk on a lost week end who has forgotten how to do anything but drink. Sober up. Come back to reality and responsibility. Begin working again. Face up to the problems that are so pleasant to leave buried in a rosy glow of inflation, and clean them up."

On the welfare state, he says: "Quit making it possible for people to sit on their fannies and expect the government to solve all their problems for them. If farmers produce too much, let the farmers find their own way to dig themselves out. If Negroes want integration, let them prove their right to it so clearly that an overwhelming majority will be convinced. If elderly people want free medical care, let them first prove they need it, and then devise a practical and acceptable plan for providing it. If teachers want federal aid to swell their salaries, let them first show they deserve the ones they are getting by teaching Johnny to read and spell."

Need for Action

The conservative is not asking for random activity. He is seeking to put purpose and values back into life. Action itself is as much a symbol of the quest for purpose as it is a release from the frustrations of inactivity, defeat, and failure.

Man is made to act. Probably the most seminal sense in which people use the word "action" is when they speak of the "action of the heart" or other organ, or even machine, meaning "performance of its proper function," as the dictionary says. The conservative has guide lines to what that "proper function" is: Bible, Constitution, traditions, rules of his social order, experience, knowledge of what works and what doesn't, history of Western civilization, his heroes of fact and fiction.

But the conservative is not a doctrinaire. He doesn't seek to coerce action by words. He does not have a pat set of hypotheses to apply to whatever conditions come along. Instead of merely churning his intellect, the conservative seeks to apply the totality of his equipment as a man to the problems that face him, that is, to act.

Whatever vexing questions there may be in the world—on Cuba and other places where communism threatens, on integration, on labor disputes, on the Common Market and the future of Europe, on farming, on taxes, on personal and national security, on defense policy, and, in fact, all the problems and challenges that agitate our time—the liberals would have the most highly educated brainpower sit down and cogitate out the correct answers. The conservative, while not blind to the fact that some answers are more correct than others, knows that frequently the most important question is whether to *do* something or nothing.

There are problems, for instance, on which almost any action would be a more or less satisfactory answer, while inaction, in these cases, would be the one thing in the world that would aggravate them.

Often it is better to remain inactive than to do anything, as all business executives know. But, contrariwise, sometimes almost any consistent, determined course of action is better than none.

It is right here that the conservative challenge is most pointed. The conservative contends we are in such an action situation today. And he finds the liberal incapable of consistent, determined action. Under modern liberal government, the conservative says, we drift.

The liberal cannot act decisively, continues the conservative, because he lacks a center in the form of firm purpose to act from. Society, the conservative says, is falling to pieces for lack of a common set of values, a common morality—and he wants to restore what holds us together. If he can, he believes, we can do anything else within the nature of man to do. If he can't, we can do nothing further. Those things that should be glorious opportunities will become insurmountable problems. And the conservative just doesn't feel that liberalism today has the clear principles to provide this center.

The Collapse of Liberalism

Events are demonstrating that the liberal today does not know what he believes. In an essay on the United Nations in *The Liberal Papers*, Professor Wright cites "a combination of boredom, apathy and fear among Americans, especially among liberals, resulting in a government policy of drift, platitude, opportunism and wide disagreement, even among liberals who take an active interest in foreign policy." The attitude Professor Wright deplores is directly traceable to the fact that liberalism is no longer a firm doctrine, but is crumbling through its own inconsistencies and contradictions. The result is what the professor calls an "almost total confusion among liberals" that indicates that "liberals do not know their values, the kind of world suitable for the realization of those values, the contribution which the United Nations might make toward establishing such a world, and what specific policies the United States government should pursue to these ends. . . ."

From Quincy Wright to Clarence Streit—yes, perhaps even including the bored supersophisticates Arthur Schlesinger and J. Kenneth Galbraith—the liberals have given us due warning of their own inner collapse. Liberal theory and liberal policy are hanging together by a thread. The liberal grasp of political power is even more tenuous, with one segment or other of liberal popular support tending to melt away with every move they make.

The liberal was never cut out to be a leader or a decision maker. He is a man of thought, a man of science, a man of books. Put him in the seats of the mighty, and he knows no better than to try to deal with the challenges he finds there, which are basically problems of people, in the same way he is accustomed to work with ideas. The liberal can plan, communicate, consult, modify, and adjust very well indeed. But he does not make decisions well. He is even poorer when it comes to leadership and action. Faced with the conditions of an era rapidly becoming postmodern, the modern liberal collapses.

Extent of the Liberal Collapse

A major theme of this book has been the nature and extent of the collapse of liberalism. But we have not yet made clear how utter, how final, we believe it to be. Liberalism today is like a hollow shell, from which the content has been drained away. It still keeps up the pretense of believing in liberal policies and **of seeking to expand liberal programs.** And we do not question

but that the liberal *would like* to believe in them—or even that
he thinks he does.

But liberal integrity has been the main victim of the underlying conservative revolution of our times. The grand liberal
plans just do not work out. To keep himself from being totally
ineffective, the liberal has had to adopt illiberal means to gain
his liberal ends. This fact lies behind much of the self-criticism
of Professor Wright and the other liberals who are becoming
increasingly conscious of the confused state liberalism is working itself into.

Manned by liberals, the Kennedy-Johnson administration must
rely more and more on hated Madison-Avenue-type buildups of
the president to retain power. That outrages all the ancient
principles of liberalism. So does the vote stealing practiced in big
cities dominated by boss-ridden political machines. So does
"news management," which is contrary to all liberal precepts on
freedom of the press and truth in information. So does pressure
politics and arm twisting.

Or take the racial question. In desperately trying to hold together the two sources of its support, both of which it apparently
believes to be indispensable, the pattern of liberal administrations seems to be to first cater to the Negro and antagonize the
South, and then cater to the South and antagonize the Negro. And in both cases the means they adopt are illiberal.
Thus the government liberals seem to have instructed government bureaus and other satrapies under their jurisdiction to show
favoritism to Negroes in hiring, and at the same time to have
ordered Democratic governors and Democratic congressmen to
vote part of the time in the interests of "party harmony," which
in this case means against antisegregation measures. Both strategies are contrary to ancient liberal principles, which stressed
freedom, justice, and equality.

By the early 1960s what had been known as "liberalism"
had become a mass of contradictions. With each succeeding
move of the Kennedy-Johnson administration these contradic-

tions got steadily worse. Like the cancer victim consumed by his own cells, liberalism was destroying itself.

Liberalism, as we have seen, originally started out in a search for freedom. Somewhere along the way it concluded that the way to enlarge freedom was through socialism and greater government control, which made it sympathetic to the doctrines of Karl Marx and the Russian Revolution of 1917. Now in the 1960s the governmental side of liberalism is saying: "Coexist with communism. The essential part of communism is governmentalization, which is just what we need." But the part of liberalism that still believed in freedom noted the slavery, oppression, and tyranny of communism, and held up its hands in helpless disgust.

The governmentalization side of liberalism said: "Let us force the whites to give in to the Negroes." The democratic (small *d*) side shied away in horror from undertaking what might well prove to be permanent compulsion of the white majority.

The liberal advocates of governmentalization said: "Let us accept the prospect of large-scale technological unemployment due to automation, and simply pension off the people it converts into incompetents." The humanitarian part of liberalism recoiled at the idea of trampling the basic human craving for self-respect.

The collapse of liberalism is double: its internal contradictions are breaking it up while its external inadequacy is condemning it to impotence. In the most basic sense the conservative challenge is not the one the conservative throws down to liberalism, but rather to threatened world collapse and communism, which the continuing degradation of liberalism is bringing with it. The head-on collision with liberalism is but the first battle that a revived conservatism must fight. Conservatism cannot even get at the real enemy—the decline of morality and character—until the liberal mystique, which grows more dense as the liberal collapse proceeds, is cleared out of the way.

Man vs. Liberal

One of the most basic liberal doctrines is that harmony among all people is possible, that there are no irreconcilable differences. Believing this with all their heart, the liberals have weakened the social fabric designed to keep irreconcilable differences from mortally injuring society. One result of this weakening of the social fabric has been communism. Another has been the precipitous decline of American prestige in world affairs.

Despite the experience of the postwar years, the liberal is still insisting that all is—or at least should be—harmony. He is still saying that if we remove all the elements that call for discipline and sternness, we can achieve world-wide cooperation without too much difficulty. And these "disciplinary elements," of course, include the very social apparatus that is able to contain conflict and competition when it does break out, keeping it from becoming destructive. One example is the free market system, which channels and restricts as well as facilitates the inevitable competition among men. Another example is the balanced budget, which, by decreeing what can and what cannot be done, makes individuals who run government accountable for their actions. Still another is maintaining the difference between success and failure—threatened by welfare-state-type thinking, which provides society with elementary ground rules for both cooperation and competition.

If the liberals are wrong in their assumption that, under their guidance mankind can and will achieve harmony, their measures will only deprive us of our defenses against disaster. As a very specific case in point, take the late President Kennedy's suspension of U-2 intelligence flights over Cuba. In mid-August 1963, at least, the United States was totally in the dark whether Khrushchev was again bringing rockets into position on his outlying island, ninety miles from the United States. And again, this is not because the liberals "trust" Khrushchev. Again and again liberals assure us that we can only "trust" the Soviet to do what is in its own best interests. No, the liberals simply believe, so firmly that they will not listen to any counterargument, that when it comes to world peace the interests of the rulers of Russia march with our own interests, and that all of us, being reasoning folk, see these interests alike.

The conservative doesn't believe this for a minute. Not only does he find an irreconcilable conflict between communism and freedom, but he also contends that, while all men and governments are combative in nature, the communists are the most quarrelsome in the world. The split between China and Russia, for instance, is a strong hint that not even in the communists' own camp can there be coexistence as long as communism remains in the world.

The conservative point of view has historically been based on the teachings of Christianity. The Psalmist sternly warned of woe to those who "cry peace, peace, when there is no peace." Christian peace is not the peace of man but the peace of God. Christ said that He "came not to bring peace but a sword."

The American people overwhelmingly disapprove of the welfare state—even though substantial minorities, or even majorities, endorse the specific measures that go to make it up. The American people are willing to bear heavier taxes, if necessary, in order to prevent deficit spending, not because they like taxes, but because they realize deficit spending is unbearably loose. The American people want a strong, forthright foreign policy, not because they want to be international dictators, but because soft policies are also slack policies. Americans want tightly enforced measures against communism, crime, immorality, vice, pornography, not simply because these are bad ideas, but because, if unchecked, they will corrupt the people.

Liberal "Perfection"

To the conservative looseness is unbearable. The liberal can tolerate it and even go out of his way to invite it, however, because he believes man to be good and perfectible. He is always seeking perfection. This combination of actual looseness and expected perfection makes him almost impossible to live with. The liberal always has the air of expecting people to be something they are not and cannot be. Marital unhappiness results from this—specifically, from the inability of the man to recognize that his wife is a woman in invisible as well as visible ways, and cannot be expected to react as a man would. For their part, the wives who have been infected by liberalism seem to expect their husbands to behave as a perfect woman would, had she the sexual equipment of a man. Unhappiness as well as failure is usually the result of unreal expectations.

Probably the basic reason a liberal makes a poor manager is that he seems constitutionally incapable of working with his men as they are, but insists on dealing with them in accordance with his mental picture of what an ideal subordinate (or superior, for that matter) would be like. Like husbands and wives in difficulties, the liberal manager doesn't see real people, but only ideas—which *are* perfectible.

Similarly with a liberal president. He fails so often because the problems he deals with are really problems of people and he doesn't see people—whether heads of foreign nations or his own constituents, whether minority groups, farmers, businessmen, labor leaders, or simply voters—as they are, but as he thinks they should be. Liberals see people as they are *not*.

The Challenge of Conservatism

The liberal gets to be the way he is largely because he is bound and determined that man (and his instrumentalities, especially government) can do anything. When our major problems were economic, he seemed to be able to pull it off. But now with our main problems those of international peace, racial discord, unemployment and automation, conflicting personal aims and ambitions, the liberal is finding that government, unless used as a weapon of coercion, is really very limited in what it can accomplish. And, with his theories crashing down around him, the liberal stands helpless.

The conservative, noting the liberal's bafflement, and realizing that something must be done, now boldly steps up and asserts he can succeed where the liberal has failed. He offers to meet the challenge of our times. The challenge *to* conservatism is one of building a new world order based on the ancient principles of Christianity. The challenge *of* conservatism is that these principles can and should be used to meet head-on and overcome what the liberal calls our "problems."

The liberal maintains that the foremost problem is the prevention of war. "Not so," says the conservative. "Prevention of war is not within the province of men to deal with." Instead, man must focus attention on the challenge of preparedness, by which men and nations make themselves strong and alert enough to discourage attack; the challenge of trust, by which men and nations seek to build up mutual trust and confidence; the challenge of definition, by which those who might provoke war are encouraged to define their ultimate goals; and the challenge of accomplishment, by which methods of attaining these goals by means other than war are explored. As long as attention is focused directly on the prevention of war, we are lost. Man *is* basically a warlike creature—and the more he pretends to be a superman who can determine issues of war and peace, the more likely war is to break out.

The Principles of Conservatism

In Chapter 3, we examined the principles of modern liberalism, and found them to be an inconsistent hodge-podge. We implied there that the creed of the conservative, on the other hand, was not only consistent, but also universally applicable (at least in Christendom), workable in practice, and interpreted in the same way by all or nearly all conservatives. In that chapter, our concern was with *economic* principles. Let us list here the four main over-all principles of conservatism, principles that are so interrelated that they are difficult to disentwine even for the purpose of analysis. They are—

1. The principle of individual responsibility.
2. The principle of strength.
3. The principle of order.
4. The principle of moderation and gradualness.

There is, it should be made clear, no principle in conservatism either of freedom or of acknowledgment of dependence on God. Both of these are too basic, too pervasive and implicit in conservatism, to be even separated out as principles. "Individual responsibility" would be a travesty without freedom of choice; "strength" is strength only where there is freedom to develop one's own character and rely on it; "order" implies an order greater than man himself can create; by seeking "moderation and gradualness," a man is tacitly admitting that he is not aiming at a utopia fashioned by his own brain and passions, but is only utilizing himself to help bring to pass what God seems to have in store for him and his fellows.

Responsible Individualism

As we have said before, the conservative believes the adult man or woman should bear the responsibility for his own life and everything that happens because of it. The responsible individual makes himself the elastic that connects what is to what ought to be. The concept "individual" performs the same role for the conservative that "idea" does for the liberal.

For the liberal, "right" and "wrong" are ideas, and those who do wrong because they didn't develop the right ideas should not be held responsible. Thus the liberal excuses the criminal because of his environment, his parents, his heredity, or just because he "didn't have a chance." The conservative excuses nobody. If the criminal didn't develop responsibility, and especially if he *can't* develop responsibility, he becomes, in conservative eyes, less than an individual because that is what an individual is: a unit of responsibility.

In punishing the criminal, the conservative is, of course, protecting society. But further than that, he is seeking the salvation of the criminal, which is for the criminal to assume responsibility for his misdeeds. In 1963, a television play appeared in the series called "The Defenders" about a convicted murderer who, many years later, was up for parole. By all accounts, he had become a completely new man. In his examination before the parole board, he fulfilled all the requirements but one: he wouldn't say he was sorry. He was a true liberal: he had become a "good" man but wouldn't acknowledge personal responsibility. Responsibility is too binding; it interferes with the freedom of the liberal. Responsibility is a kind of obedience, with a hint of authority about it—and obedience and authority are what the liberal wants to be liberated from.

Once upon a time, personal responsibility was comparatively unnecessary, and what little there was of it was fairly simple.

Under feudalism, loyalty to lord, family, friends, and vassals was all the "responsibility" one needed. If one wasn't loyal, retribution was usually quick in coming.

Responsible individualism has grown out of loyalty. But it is so much more complex that it is almost unrecognizable. Today, to do what one's superior tells one to do, or what it is traditional to do, is not enough; the responsible man in a republic must act without being told. Nor is it enough to be inertly "good." The most important crimes of today are the crimes of omission rather than of commission.

The major ingredient of responsibility is initiative. Crimes occur not because of initiative, but because of the lack of it; the criminal just doesn't have the gumption to keep from crime. He commits crime the way nations stumble and stagger into war. No wonder both refuse to admit responsibility. Crime and insanity, like aggression in war, are almost solely limited to the irresponsible, who should not be treated like human beings because they are *not* human beings.

The Principle of Strength

An individual who accepts responsibility for his own life develops moral strength. A man or woman of moral strength is individually responsible. The two principles are, in a very real sense, restatements of each other. But they concentrate the emphasis differently.

It has been a long time since America judged an issue on the basis of its contribution to strength or weakness of character. And yet that is the most important criterion of all. Deficit spending may or may not lead to financial catastrophe, but its implications of getting something for nothing are surely ruining our national willingness to subject ourselves, either as individuals or as a people, to any sort of discipline. The welfare state may or may not deal in true welfare but there is no doubt at all that it is undermining our self-reliance. Such government undergirding of economic groups as the farm program may or may not help to alleviate economic problems, but it does hold back members of the particular economic segment from devising and putting into execution their own solutions. Coexistence with communism may or may not be the way to peace in our time, but it certainly would contribute to a feeling that "anything goes," and make still more flabby our national hold on any absolute morality.

The principle of strength has its applications both to domestic and international problems. It is no accident that Barry Goldwater, with his cry of "Why not victory!" in foreign affairs, should advocate measures designed to strengthen the individual at home. The two approaches to strength meet in nationalism, since the strong person is the person who takes pride in his world (including his family, his religion, his country), and the essence of nationalism (sometimes erroneously referred to as "isolationism") is a man's confidence in the moral strength of his country.

The Principle of Order

Order is necessarily based on strength. This can best be appreciated, perhaps, by trying to imagine a society in which the honors would go to those who flaunt weakness, rewards would be achieved by failing, and positions of greatest responsibility would be filled by the insane.

The principle of order is essentially an acceptance of the idea that the world is God's world and not man's, and that it is run by His rules, one of which is that strength, success, victory, honor, life, and virtue are to be sought, and weakness, failure, defeat, dishonor, death, and vice avoided. Another is that the elements of order must be imposed by the individual through his power to choose, not by government or machine.

The Principle of Moderation and Gradualness

It used to be taken for granted that if a man is a conservative he is opposed to any abrupt, violent, or hasty change; that he seeks to avoid all extremes; and that he bends his influence to promote the gradual and the temperate. And this assumption, so often mislaid in the present day, is right.

Here again the four principles of conservatism can hardly be separated. Moderation and gradualness imply an orderly approach to all things, never upheaval. Strength will always be found on the side of the moderate and the gradual; only the weak want a revolution in all things—and the more responsible an individual is, the less he will permit himself to go to extremes or to start something he might not be able to finish.

The well-known conservative attachment to limited government falls under this principle. While extremism is by definition an attempt to push the permissible limits further and further out, moderation seeks to draw them within known and explored territory, and to make them as compatible as possible with the rules governing man and society as tested and proved by experience.

The Challenge of the Postmodern Era

One of the most successful of the liberal hoaxes has been either to downgrade these conservative principles or deny that they *are* conservative. The only conservative principle his opposite number seems willing to recognize is the principle of the *status quo*. Too, the liberal contends that conservatism is the philosophy of money and materialism, and liberalism the philosophy of human values. The greatest hoax of all is the liberal argument that liberalism, and not conservatism, is suited to the conditions of the world of the future.

Just the opposite is true. In the latter half of the twentieth century, more so than in the preceding century and a half, the need is, and will be increasingly, for the strength of character that conservatism fosters and promotes. Times will be rough— too rough for the tender-minded liberal—despite all possible economic and social gains. The later twentieth century will be featured by tensions in profession and employment, tensions in the family, political and social tensions, and, above all, international tensions. These tensions will be signs of a basic disorder in the world.

Problems of "mental health" that the liberals are so concerned about have become acute precisely because the liberals have climbed into jobs that are too big for them, and which they are rapidly losing control of. Without control, social, political, or economic, the world has already slid a long way toward hell. Even if the conservatives regain power tomorrow, to put the country and world back together will take a long, long time. Even under the best conditions that can reasonably be expected to develop, the individual will have to bear strains never before known in the history of the world. The liberal would go to pieces under them. Only the conservative can "take it," because, after all, those who do willingly and uncomplainingly "take" what the world dishes out *are* conservatives. The conservative may not have strength to begin with, but he develops it. The world the conservative finds himself in may be disorderly, but he reduces it to order. Extremist tendencies may operate toward producing deep divisive clefts, but the conservative somehow contrives to hold both himself and his world together.

Liberalism has already destroyed much of the connective tissue of society. If, even during a period of repair, society stays together, it will only be because the conservatively responsible individual absorbs the tensions and strains into his own personality.

This may well be the only way in which the world will survive into the postmodern era. In the name of the responsible individual, the conservative, rising to the occasion, accepts the challenge and throws down one of his own.

CHAPTER ELEVEN

The Coming Victory of Conservatism

Conservative victory at the polls could come in 1964. If not then, in 1968. The basic reason? Liberalism has degenerated into failure, failure such as is revealed in such headlines as the following:

PRESIDENT'S CUBAN TROUBLES TO WORSEN—AT HOME, ABROAD

WESTERN AID PROGRAM IN DANGER OF COLLAPSE

NORTH RACIAL TENSIONS RISE

PARIS—PEKING LINK UNHINGES WASHINGTON'S CHINA POLICY

JOHNSON, HOME, SPLIT OVER CUBA

INQUIRY UNCOVERS FLAW IN RANGER 6

EXILES REPORT NEW RUSSIAN BASES IN CUBA

PANAMA BREAKS U.S. RELATIONS, DEMANDS SURRENDER OF CANAL

ZANZIBAR SEIZES U.S. ENVOYS AT GUNPOINT

And the American people, whatever their understanding of the intellectual niceties anent liberalism and conservatism, do not like failure.

Liberal Failure, Fumbling and Fear

In foreign policy, the liberals have failed. In spite of our tremendous economic power, in spite of America's actual and potential leadership in leading the world to higher standards of living, in spite of the world-wide appeal of the unvarnished American personality, and in spite of the American warmhearted sympathy with the oppressed and underprivileged, our official softness and lack of resolve are almost creating a power vacuum where America should stand.

NATO is in disarray; France and England and other nations that should be close American allies are being forced to forage independently; we repay our smaller foreign supporters by conniving at their murder (as in the case of South Vietnam's Diem and Nhu); by our weak and ambiguous policies we encourage other small nations to stick pins in us (as in Cuba and Panama) and respond by making ourselves "self-sufficient" (as in the case of the Castroite shut-off of water at Guantanamo Bay); we aid and encourage our enemies and punish our friends (as when we forced the former pro-Western government of Laos to dilute itself with communists and neutralists, or pro-Western Katanga to surrender to the central Congo government).

In race relations the liberals have failed. A racial minority, at liberal urging, is trying to force the majority to bow to its will, sowing the seeds of friction for centuries to come. During these future centuries, the center of the problem could well shift from the South to the great cities of the North.

In economic policy, the liberals have failed. After thirty years of inflation, our economy today is a bubble that has been blown to its fullest. Our job today is to strengthen it. Instead, the liberals are trying to blow it up yet more. Concealed by inflation, defense and welfare spending, and high taxes, our basic economic problems are still unsolved and are becoming more acute than ever. In an artificial price-and-wage system, production and consumption are no longer in balance. There is little incentive to take the risks inseparable from economic initiative. Most dramatic of all, the unregulated and quickened pace of automation, coupled with easy tolerance for those who drop out of school assured that the government will look after them, are turning more and more of our people into unemployables.

In social policy, the liberals have made the greatest failure of all, because it is the cause of all the rest. The liberals believe government can do it all, that individuals can "go along" for a free ride. The liberals believe that weakness can be substituted for strength of character and determination. As the result of the debilitation of the American character, moral standards have fallen to a new low, pornography accosts our children at every newsstand, the ravages of crime and drunkenness and mental illness are burning deeper and deeper scars, the people are becoming wholesale victims of tensions, unhappiness, and confusion.

The Cause

Why these failures? Because liberals do not understand the nature of man. Liberal idealism is not undergirded with realism. Liberal economic and political theory is not supported by a firm grasp on moral truth and a deep sense of religion. As a consequence, liberals cannot help but fumble, piling up both errors and enemies in an age when skilled human relations are more important than ever before. In human relations the liberal doesn't get to first base. He doesn't seem able to realize that there are basic moral yearnings and even "prejudices" of man that cannot be ignored or glossed over.

In earlier eras, liberal fumbling was often concealed from public inspection. But today, all of us who "keep in touch" know, at least subconsciously, both that our liberal government is erratic and indecisive, and that if continued this lack of clear direction could be fatal. And the conservatives have at last become articulate enough to begin showing that this fumbling is not written in the stars, but rather is the product of liberalism. Liberalism, recognizing its own weakness, is in no hurry to meet the challenge conservatism is throwing down, but when the head-on collision does take place, there will be no doubt how the American people will vote.

The Common Sense of Conservatism

The whole liberal position has been derived from sophistication, which has steadily increased since Occam and has now, among the most advanced liberals, reached incredible heights.

In contrast, the conservative stand is so simple, so immersed in common sense and experience, that it may seem almost static. "The principles on which the conservative political position is based," says Senator Goldwater, "have been established by a process that has nothing to do with the social, economic and political landscape that changes from decade to decade and from century to century. . . Circumstances do change. So do the problems that are shaped by circumstances. But the principles that govern the solution of the problems do not. . . . The conservative approach is nothing more or less than an attempt to apply the wisdom and the experience and the revealed truths of the past to the problems of today."

That is to say, the conservative approach is nothing more or less than an attempt to apply common sense. Even the basis of morality is common sense—and the basis of common sense is morality. For what is either but the ability to learn by listening, living, and doing, and to apply that learning to new living in such a way that the individual grows and at the same time society becomes firmer and more stable?

The human infant, at least in conservative eyes, is not endowed at birth with the ability to take care of himself, let alone others. *Only* "the wisdom and experience and the revealed truths of the past" can teach him. And however old he grows, and however high and mighty he thinks he has become, he will never outgrow the need to sit at the feet of this teacher and accept tradition and folklore from the past, even if the liberals tell him he humiliates himself in doing so.

The liberal thinks he can cut loose from the past when he perceives it as hard or cruel or unjust. But our present predicament shows us, ever more clearly, that we cannot. Even government cannot give us immunity from being what we are—creatures of mixed good and evil—and only the lessons of the past can show us how to keep the evil down and bring out the good. We *must* pin our hope to what has been proved to work out, not to a will-o'-the-wisp. And since in human terms a thing is really proved only by experience, we *must* maintain our continuity with the past or we lose all. We cannot trade common sense for utopia, no matter how brilliantly conceived or how well deserved. We cannot build an enduring idealism except on the firm basis of realism.

Wallets and Ideals

But liberals, as this book has already said so many times and in so many different ways, think we can. Liberalism was, in the beginning, highly idealistic. Whatever was "not right" (that is, "not right" in their opinion) should, the liberals thought, be done away with, and done away with instantly.

It was no mere coincidence that modern American liberalism started in 1913. The years immediately preceding World War I were probably the period of the greatest idealism in our history. They were years of muckraking, reform, trustbusting, progressivism. Optimism ran high too, and unlike the optimism of the 1920s, that of the turn of the century seemed to ring true. Anything seemed possible.

The situation was just right for liberalism. It stepped boldly into its first great military venture in 1917. We were off to "make the world safe for democracy," to fight a war to end all wars, to build "freedom and justice and self-government amongst all the nations of the world." There was substantial self-interest in our support of Britain and France that led to our entry into war: Anglo-French loans, purchases of munitions, expanded markets for farm produce. But the economic motives by themselves would never have brought us into war. We entered that war because of liberal idealism.

The conclusion of the war, the repudiation of Wilson, and the failure of his Fourteen Points, the saga of the ill-fated League of Nations, and the disastrous course of postwar Europe destroyed the first rosy glow of the liberal patina, but the liberal mystique itself hung on. We have been living under its pall ever since.

During the twenties, we elected as president, first Harding, then Coolidge, then Hoover. Liberal fantasy has it that all three were conservatives, but Harding and Coolidge were neuter. They hardly even attempted to restore our prewar character. Both insisted on our adherence to the World Court. In government affairs, Coolidge *was* an economizer, but he stubbornly refused to take steps to bring back sound credit to the economy. Inflation, encouraged by the loose policies of the Federal Reserve Board, kept the country a land of unreality.

By the time Herbert Hoover took office as president, the inflation had gotten out of hand, and the ensuing crash and depression panicked the people. Franklin Roosevelt took advantage of this panic to resort to more liberalism to cure the problem liberalism had caused. In a way he succeeded: he restored inflationary conditions, which swept some of the recession, by then grown into depression, under the rug.

By 1939, the props had been knocked out from under our economy, which was left to float on liberal air. After 1941, under the cloak first of winning a new war and then of saving the peace, the liberals continued undermining our constitutional heritage, not only in economics, but politically, socially, constitutionally. In so doing, they themselves are the first to be destroyed. Timbers are falling, all right, but they are falling on the liberals.

Liberalism had flourished in the World War I era because self-interest marched in the same direction as liberal idealism. It flourished during the depression for the same reason, only more so; the programs of the New Deal were regarded as making jobs, bringing back prosperity, providing money and security. But after 1936 doubts began to grow. Liberalism brought subsidies and handouts, the people knew, but it also brought inflation, high taxes, corruption and war—and a curious type of lassitude.

By 1952, these doubts had become grave enough to result in the election of a Republican president. In many ways, President Eisenhower was not a conservative, but his eight years did see political liberalism taking to its deathbed. President Kennedy was not able to restore it to more than feeble existence. The New Frontier has been more like a rest home for the sick and infirm. And why? Because by that time liberal idealism and the liberal optimism, both of which had been growing shallower, had already been our guiding philosophy for a half century. And it was becoming obvious that the interests of the people and liberal theories were not on the same side. Liberalism did not solve problems; it brought more. Each of the six minorities that had supported liberal power for so long were beginning to recognize this. Let us examine these six, one by one, starting with the Negro minority.

Negro vs. Liberal

The long flirtation between Negro and liberal will, in the end, bring disaster to both sides. The Negro wants results—and the liberal is constitutionally unequipped to produce results. Undoubtedly he tries, but in this, as in all other cases, the liberal just doesn't know how to go about being successful. In this particular matter, it is becoming more and more apparent that forced physical "integration" will bring about a greater degree of moral segregation than ever.

The most tragic aspect of the whole matter may be that the Negro, after all, does not want "integration" into white society and its values. On the contrary, the Negro, like all the rest of us, wants most to live his or her own life in the way that fits best the unique characteristics of the individual Negro.

And the alliance is turning out to be even more ruinous to the liberal. As early as 1963 it had become evident that sponsorship of the Negro cause was breaking up the liberal coalition of minorities. Southerners were appalled by the threat of coercion, which would overturn their traditional social patterns. Jews were beginning to resent the fact that while they themselves had had to earn economic and social acceptance the hard way, the Negro was being sheltered by government favoritism—and was expecting more; anti-Semitism was becoming fashionable among the Negroes. The northern groups most disaffected on the Negro question were the Irish, Mexican-Americans, and perhaps the Poles—all Catholics. The less well-educated found themselves in competition for jobs with the Negro, and resented the fact the Negro seemed so often to have the inside track. Employment sections of the Civil Rights Bill of 1964 were directed against union discrimination as much or more than against discrimination by employers; here was an issue on which lifelong Democratic union men could part company with their leaders, perhaps even to the extent of voting against the liberals. The race question by itself could be converting the famous liberal coalition of minorities into a shambles.

If the race problem had only been realistically outlined and tackled twenty or thirty years ago—say, if Franklin Roosevelt had tackled it—most of the uproar about "integrated schooling" and "public accommodations" could have been avoided at the cost of providing Negro organizations with only a small portion of the funds lavished on such governmental projects as foreign aid. Even part of a billion dollars would set up a great many training facilities for Negroes. It would also support a publicity and promotion campaign to overcome prejudice, and finance small business ventures for the Negro.

Instead, the liberals, always intent on spending money for the wrong things, and inept at any kind of human relations, aggravated the irritations of the Negroes themselves, and fumbled us to the verge of race war. When in 1963, James Baldwin, the Negro novelist, and a group of other Negro leaders met with Attorney General Robert Kennedy, they were amazed by what, pityingly, they could only call his "extreme naïveté." In commenting on this meeting, columnist Joseph Alsop, who usually defends the liberal point of view, noted that, whatever may have been the case in the past, Negro extremism today is fed, not by injustice, but by concessions. "Leaders," he says, "who were moderate in the era of the iron hand become very passionate indeed in the era of the velvet glove." Is it not strange for Alsop, purported to be a liberal, to notice in domestic policy the same phenomenon that conservatives have been citing with regard to the appeasement of international communism?

In Chapter 6, we saw that, strange as it may seem, communist leaders could deal better with the conservatives, who hate communism, than with the liberals, who are willing to coexist with it. In the same way, Negroes may come to see that they can profit more from a conservative environment than from liberalism, even though the latter bleeds for them.

Southerner vs. Liberal

After the forced integration of Ole Miss and the University of Alabama, and the Birmingham riots, the South—possibly even including the Negro South—is irretrievably lost to the liberals, whatever they do—except, possibly, if the liberal candidate for president happens to be a southerner. The long era of a "solid Democratic South" was ended by the looseness of the liberals and their inability to understand men.

And this loose thinking, as fate would have it, was demonstrated on the South's most sensitive problem. "Integrate," the liberals said, "and everything will be all right." "Integration," to the typical liberal, is only a word, as both southern whites and Negroes observe to their consternation. The liberal's grand attitude toward race problems, with its tendency to overlook the individual in observing the mass, has so muddled the issues that there is no telling now just what the true feeling in the South toward segregation is. Before the Kennedy administration, southern support of segregation was declining. But no Americans like to be dictated to. As a result of armed intervention, there may be more anti-Negro feeling in the South today than at any time since Reconstruction.

Nevertheless, the South is not fighting for segregation, which almost all feel is a doomed institution. It is fighting for law and order. The South is fighting liberal dictation that would pry up its whole moral and social code, and expose southern society nakedly to violence and lawlessness of the kind that broke out in 1963. It is seeking to avoid a period of looseness, in which neither the whites nor the Negroes know where they stand, and which would almost inevitably erupt into bloodshed.

Because of the preoccupation with civil rights and the South's traumatic feeling about its ability to handle its own problems of race relations, attention has been diverted from the significance of the fact that the South is our most conservative region. While ordinarily conservatism and segregation have little in common, in this one instance they do. Southern conservatism centers on the dread of what might happen in areas where the white population is outnumbered, or nearly so, by the Negroes.

It would be one thing if the liberals had a new plan to deal with situations, as old as man, where two radically different points of view confront each other. But they don't. All they seem to know how to do is to destroy the system of authority that has grown up in the South. Admittedly grossly imperfect, it is still the best the South has. And with reason southerners fear its destruction will lead only to authority-less chaos.

Catholic vs. Liberal

Catholics and liberals are natural enemies. Their unnatural alliance cannot long survive any extended effort to exercise joint power. The liberals favor birth control, both national and world wide; opposition to birth control is at the heart of Roman Catholicism. Liberals want to undermine Catholic schools; to this bitter enmity they are willing even to sacrifice one of their favorite nostrums: federal aid to education. The National Education Association, for instance, seems to prefer no federal aid at all to the prospect that Catholic schools might be aided too. Liberals are against prayers even in public schools; Catholics are determined that the religious element should not be removed from education. Liberals are one-world-minded; Catholics, despite their reverence for the Pope, are perhaps our most nationalistic religious group.

Liberalism began as an attempt to pry loose from Catholic dogma. The centuries have seen one head-on collision after another between liberalism and Catholicism. The warfare is too bitter to be long glossed over by the personality of a Catholic president, no matter who he may have been. In the long run, the Catholic will line up against the liberal.

Labor vs. Liberal

The issue in labor, Eric Severeid says, "is becoming less and less one of wages and working conditions, and more and more one of fundamental job security, as the implacable movement of technology changes the whole nature of man's work in this country. . . . The real ghost," he continues, "is automation. . . . Whole trades, ancient skills, are at stake, not just jobs."

In the revolution of automation, labor unions are in for the fight of their lives—and a fight for which they are not prepared. Mr. Severeid doesn't think they will make it. He thinks labor will lose out to government, which will then take over. Maybe. Nevertheless, the unions are bound to try. And in this fight, as Severeid implies, the antagonist will not be management at all. It will be government itself.

Signs of coming strife between the labor unions and liberal government intellectuals are already appearing. This new trend was shown in the labor disaffection for Arthur Goldberg, former counsel for the United Steelworkers of America, both as Secretary of Labor and as Supreme Court Justice. It was inherent in a blast by Paul Jacobs, labor organizer and official turned writer/intellectual, attacking not only his old boss David Dubinsky, president of the International Ladies Garment Workers' Union, but labor leadership in general. Liberal TV commentator David Susskind has vented his spleen on James Carey, president of the International Union of Electrical Workers, and Murray Kempton, former columnist for the liberal New York *Post*, was outraged by the long New York newspaper strike by the International Typographical Union. The fight against the government liberals' desire to do business with the communists is led by the International Longshoremen's Union.

On the issues that caused the liberal outbursts, such as the 35-hour week, restrictive labor practices, strikes, management is not likely to leap to the defense of labor unions. But business management, being primarily concerned with the management of people, at least comes closer to appreciating the real feelings of the individual working man than do liberals, who think grandly (and loosely) in terms of large ideas—and, of course, politics.

Even in the absence of the Negro question, a steadily widening split between the working man and the liberal intellectuals would have been all but inevitable. The working man, for instance, did not wildly cheer President Johnson's plan to discourage overtime, which sometimes increased his pay by a third to a half or more. There are fewer and fewer things a liberal administration can do to endear itself to the hearts of blue- (and white-) collar men, but a great many things it can do to antagonize them.

Less Well Educated vs. Liberal

Generally the better educated the voter, the less likely he is to vote Democratic. College-trained voters are much more likely to be Republican than are high-school graduates, and usually the latter are more Republican (or less Democratic) than grade-school graduates.

However, there is an exception. Although those who went only to grade school voted more than two to one for Truman over Dewey, they split almost evenly on Stevenson four years later. Truman was a man the less well educated could take to their hearts; Stevenson wasn't. Most of the grade-school graduates were hard workers, and practically all work with their hands. They were alienated by the big words and loose intellectual concepts of Adlai Stevenson.

As a matter of fact, in early 1964 it appeared to be this very group in which there would be the greatest number of defectors. Most of these men and women are characterized by a rugged morality that tends to be outraged by deficit spending and related liberal policies; by an unsophisticated hankering for a determined foreign policy as against our present gutless one; and by what the liberals would call "prejudices"—strong racial and religious opinions; resistance to shipping economic aid overseas when "there is so much need at home"; dislike of fine-spun intellectuality; distrust of concentration of wealth and power in Washington, and so on.

But, important as all these factors can be at times, they do not pack such a punch as an issue involving jobs—an issue that this group is especially sensitive to. It is on this point and with this group that Johnson, just as did Dewey and Stevenson for more general reasons, may meet his Waterloo. For these are the very people who feel most threatened, as we have said, by the job-favoritism being shown to the Negro. And they are the ones already hard hit by the shortage of unskilled jobs and the onrush of technological unemployment—two areas that seem to have the liberals helplessly paralyzed.

The Jews vs. the Liberals

During the years since Roosevelt, the Jews have tended to vote overwhelmingly liberal. But this vote is beginning to erode; in the four years between 1958 and 1962 it went down from 84 per cent Democratic to 72 per cent Democratic, or one seventh. Jews, like the rest of us, realize that the liberals in power in 1962 didn't know what they were doing. Moreover, the modern Jew is faced with a rapidly changing situation embodying at least three new elements: (1) the most important anti-Semitism is now in communist countries that the liberals want to coexist with; (2) the danger to Israel is that, as the Moslem world, helped by economic aid from a liberal United States Government, penetrates more and more deeply into the leadership vacuum of the African continent, and consolidates its position in the Near East, Israel will simply be squeezed out; and (3) as the liberals make politics supreme over economics, the potentials of anti-Semitism in the United States will increase. At the moment, liberalism is anti-anti-Semitic. But as monolithic government grows stronger and more all encompassing, the possibility of loose thinking, scapegoat hunting, and discrimination likewise grows.

In an economic environment, most Jews seem well able to take care of themselves. What they have to fear is precisely the politically driven, head-on-collisionless welfare state now being developed by the liberals, which gives the power to those who can dominate politically, and who sometimes turn out to be anti-

Semites. Although the Jews have done so much to nourish liberalism, nevertheless, they have more to fear than any other group from the loosely-hung-together Leviathan it has developed into, whether it remains, as now, a collection of goodhearted though rather irresponsible fumblers, or whether it is taken over by a gang of power-crazed scoundrels.

The Liberal Gives Up

The liberals themselves admit that the people are turning against them. In listing the supporters of "extreme conservatism," Seymour Lipset, in his essay in *The Radical Right*, lumps together the following:

1. People who belong to such "filiopietistic organizations as the Daughters of the American Revolution, the Colonial Dames, veterans' organizations, historical commemoration societies, patriotic groups, etc."

2. "The man who makes money himself [and] feels aggrieved about social reform measures which involve redistribution of the wealth."

3. Low-income groups. "The lower a person is in socioeconomic status or educational attainment, the more likely he is to support McCarthyism,* favor restrictions on civil liberties and back a 'get tough' policy with the communist states."

4. "The former isolationist group, especially its German base, [which] was under a need to justify its past, and to a certain extent, to gain revenge."

5. Catholics [who] "as a religious group are more prone to support anticommunist movements than any other sect with the possible exception of the fundamentalist Protestant churches." (In passing, Lipset explains that "the current anticommunist crusade has united the two most morally and sexually inhibited

---

*This was written in 1955.

groups in America, the fundamentalist Protestants and the Irish Catholics.")

6. Women. Although his official list is limited to the above five, Lipset notes that "many of the organizations which are active in local struggles to intimidate school and library boards are women's groups." Lipset asserts that women tend, more than men, to be bigoted, and suggests that women are illiberal because they are intolerant. "Women are more religious than men," he writes, "and religious people are more likely to be intolerant than the non-religious. However, even when religious participation is held constant, women are more likely to be intolerant than are men."

When these groups are added up, and the patriots, the successes in business, the low-income group, the "former isolationists," Catholics and fundamentalist Protestants, and women (together with the farmers, whom David Riesman and Nathan Glazer in another essay acknowledge to be lost) are subtracted from liberal support, that cause cannot have too many backers left.

Liberalism's Impending Crash

The unanswered problems of liberalism began coming to a head almost as soon as Lyndon Johnson took over the presidency. To outward appearances, it looked at first as if the new President was doing all right. In early 1964, pollsters found that two-thirds or even three-fourths of the electorate thought they would vote for him rather than any Republican in sight. But pressures were rapidly building up to crack the liberal hegemony from stem to stern.

The civil-rights issue, on which President Johnson was committed to support the Negro, was taking a direction that, for sheer impact, could dwarf the peace or prosperity issues or any other in American history during the last hundred years. Whites, even (or maybe especially) in the northern cities, began to feel threatened on the three fronts that counted most: children, jobs, and home. Negro leaders were seeking to have children transported long distances to a school in another neighborhood in order to eliminate "*de facto* segregation," and to subject the sale and rental of houses and other property to government control in order to end discrimination. This, added to the favoritism shown Negroes in governmental and quasi-governmental employment policies, outraged many who formerly considered themselves pro-civil rights, and was the most inflammable of all the tinderboxes the new President found himself sitting on.

In Congress, the emergence of the Republicans as the balance of power between the northern Democrats and the southern Democrats was beginning to make clear that the GOP was the party of moderation, while the President was pushed more and more into the role of trying to hold together antagonistic extremes.

Also in Congress, President Johnson was using up reservoirs of good will at an alarming rate by his arm-twisting tactics designed to squeeze out victories on every inch of the administration position. While the President was bending every effort to move closer ideologically to the Americans for Democratic Action, even congressmen and senators affiliated with it as individuals began showing their resentment, thus proving that the human dislike of being pushed around is, in the final analysis, stronger than ideological bonds. Furthermore, individual congressmen who went down the line out of loyalty to the administration could sense the back-home effect of such votes as their Johnson-decreed opposition to the Smith amendment providing equal rights for women, or their Johnson-ordered rejection of tax relief for hard-pressed families of college students. And it made them very unhappy.

The Supreme Court, pursuing its determinedly liberal way, paradoxically dealt a stunning blow to the Democratic Party, champion of liberalism, in holding that the membership of the House of Representatives should be proportioned according to the vote. This decision alone, if enforced, could propel the Republican Party into power in that chamber. In 1960, House Republicans won 48 per cent of the vote, but largely because of gerrymandered districts received only 40 per cent of the seats. This Supreme Court decision opened up one of the most fascinating political questions of modern times. Would the liberals stand as firmly behind the Court when to do so might mean the end of their political power as they did on the desegregation question?

Defense policies were becoming one of the prickliest of the thorns in the side of the administration. Right after the President and the Secretary of Defense scolded Barry Goldwater for his temerity in even mentioning the possibility that missiles might not be too reliable, Ranger 6 spectacularly failed in its photographic mission, illustrating the unreliability of all of these tremendously complicated pieces of automation. Moreover, the scientists couldn't explain the cause of the failure—and so obviously would be unable to control a similar problem on a military missile. And a few days later an Associated Press dispatch noted that an "Athena missile misfired in its first overland test flight and spun crazily to earth in southwestern Colorado." Newspapers carried stories of other missile failures.

The final blows, according to indications in early 1964, would be delivered on the foreign fronts. Panama insisted that we give up the Panama Canal—and Washington seemed to be listening. Castro shut off drinking water to the Americans at Guantanamo Bay. From one end of the country to another, voters began asking themselves: "What's coming off here? Is America the strongest power in the world, or is it to be buffeted this way and that way by every petty dictator and chauvinist politician?"

France's De Gaulle recognized Red China, calling the liberals' bluff by which they sympathized with Red China at the same time they tried to keep their official face sternly set against her. And Britain claimed as much right to sell buses to Communist Cuba as we had to sell wheat to Communist Russia.

Possibly the most typical example of liberal infirmity was a plea of Secretary of State Dean Rusk in February 1964. The august secretary of state was in a state of indecision over the proper answer to make to nations, often our stanchest allies, who insisted on trading with Cuba. He sought to pass the buck to the man in the street by suggesting a consumers' boycott of such nations—to be entirely voluntary, of course.

A political "sleeper" that could wreck the liberals is the possibility that more of the assassination story would come out before election. The people had (or thought they had) confirmation by Chief Justice Warren that the full story was not being allowed to come out. Most Americans with opinions—and practically all foreigners with opinions—believed the late President Kennedy had been the victim of a plot that possibly involved Jack Ruby, Oswald's killer, as well as Lee Harvey Oswald, the assassin, himself. A poll in March 1964 showed that millions of Americans believed Ruby shot Oswald to keep him quiet.

Oswald was a known communist. Credible evidence of a communist plot to kill the American president would complete the destruction of the political dominance of the liberals—with their softness on communism—for many years to come, perhaps forever.

The Conservative Success

Possibly the most correct way to explain the weakening of the liberal's minorities is to say they are on the way back to being reabsorbed into the majority—or at least contenders for majority status—and that as a nation we are coming into a new era where politics once again will be dominated by an interest-majority rather than by ideological minorities.

This means that both parties once again would be basically conservative parties. In the long pull, all conservative interests will not be on the same side. But until liberalism is released from power, the conservatives will be united by the common objective of restoring the ground rules under which a free society must operate.

On the basic necessity for, and the nature of, these ground rules, old and young, city and country, the old Democratic West and South, and the old Republican East are coming closer and closer to seeing eye to eye. Let us conclude this book with a quick glance at the hammering out of new conservative majorities to replace the liberal minorities.

Age Brings Conservatism

Few things are truer in politics than that as voters reach middle age and beyond, most of them become more conservative. During the 1950s, the Survey Research Center of the University of Michigan found that only 7 or 8 per cent of eligible voters in their twenties considered themselves "strong Republicans," but that this percentage steadily increased with age, until 26 per cent of those over seventy-five did.

Many factors contribute to this phenomenon. But the most seminal one is that the longer a man lives, *if he has a reasonably open mind*, the more he realizes that conservative ideas and ways of doing things work better than do liberal ideas and methods, and are more satisfying.

We add these italicized words because the verbal support at least for liberalism seems also to grow somewhat with age. About 20 per cent of the younger voters and 25 per cent of their elders considered themselves "strong Democrats." (However, this small gain was much more than counterbalanced by the fact that the number of "weak Democrats" was cut almost in half as age increased, while the number of "weak Republicans" remained about the same, regardless of age. As age advances, the percentage actually voting Democratic gets down closer and closer to the hard core of the "strong Democrats.")

But while the older people *are* more conservative at heart, they do not always show it by voting for whatever Republican candidate is nominated. Unlike Democrats, who often vote on the basis of party loyalty, those who register as Republicans tend to cast their votes from principle or because of the personality of the candidate. The Michigan research survey team asked members of both parties how they would vote if their party was running a candidate they didn't like or agree with. Forty per cent of the "strong Democrats" said they "would probably vote for him anyway, because a person should be loyal to his party." Only 28 per cent of the "strong Republicans" would do so. The Republicans are mostly conservatives. Many of them, especially in the older-age groups, see no point in voting for a "me too" liberal candidate simply because he was sold to the Republican convention.

In 1948, only 31 per cent of the over fifty-fives voted for Dewey, with 37 per cent staying at home. Four years later, about 50 per cent voted for Eisenhower, while 23 per cent stayed home. In both years, 27 per cent voted for the Democrat. The reason for this big shrinkage of the stay-at-home vote—all of which went to the Republicans? There was more of a head-on collision between Eisenhower and Stevenson than between Dewey and Truman. True, all of Eisenhower's economic and political ideas were not conservative. But his personality certainly was. Over-all, he appealed to the conservative instincts of the voters—especially the older voters—more than Stevenson did. When the interests of the older people (nearly 30 per cent of the electorate potential are fifty-five and older) are aroused, most of the "weak Republicans," the independents, and even the "weak Democrats" can be persuaded to join the "strong Republicans" in voting Republican, while only the "strong Democrats" will vote Democratic.

Youth Becomes Conservative

While age has always been conservative, youth, which is traditionally the exponent of liberalism, is today becoming a hot-bed of conservatism. During the years since the middle 1950s a profound change has taken place in the politics of young people. Even during the four-year period 1958–62, Republicanism of those twenty-one to twenty-nine years old grew from 38 per cent to 48 per cent. Earlier in the decade of the 1950s, the Michigan survey team found that party preference by those twenty-one to twenty-four years old divided 30-70 in favor of the Democrats, which is about the same as the preference of first voters in 1940.

During roughly the decade preceding 1962, party preference by first voters changed from two and three to one against the Republicans to certainly an even split, and in the decade following 1962, it might well become two (or more) to one *for* the Republicans.

In colleges and universities, the best students are calling themselves "Young Conservatives," reading conservative books (without credit), organizing conservative clubs, publishing conservative magazines, sponsoring conservative speakers. Reversing the previous order, the Young Conservatives are organizing missionary efforts to convert their professors. They are, by far, the most lively and energetic group on many campuses. And it pays off. At Stanford, for instance, the chairmanships of three of the four student caucuses—Republican, Democratic, and Conservative—were held, in 1962, by avowed conservatives; liberals dominated only the Socialist caucus.

And when the Young Conservatives graduate, most of them become leaders of the Young Republicans (they seem to sense that there is no future with the Young Democrats). But the Young Republicans, as a group the most vocal party organ grinders for conservatism in the country, *are* the future. Not only are they young, but the Republican Party has become the home of an overwhelming majority of the college-trained. Even most of the college men who started out years before as Democrats, had, by 1964, begun to vote the Republican ticket.

Why this startling shift from the tame liberalism and social-security consciousness of youth in the early postwar years? Because today young people, full of life, vigor, and initiative, are rebelling against the idea of living out their years in an old people's home, which they now realize the liberal's welfare state to be. Young Conservatives have seen what the welfare state is doing to their elders. They don't want to be condemned to a stiffer dose of the same poison. They are brimming with energy and want a clear field for their initiative and enterprise. They are eager for risks and adventure. The fear that infected those who knew the depression has not touched them: the Young Conservatives who are twenty-four years old in 1964 were born in 1940, when the enemy was personified evil, not a debilitating phantasmagoria.

The future is being molded by the Young Conservatives just as surely as the present was hatched by the Young Socialists around the turn of the century.

The Conservative Union

Just as today young and old are being politically united by conservatism, so are country and city, east, west, north, and south. Nowhere is liberalism gaining ground.

Country people are conservative, and becoming more so. The ruralite, like the older-age groups he overlaps in a number of ways, may sometimes find his conservative instincts frustrated because of lack of opportunities to reflect it in elections. For instance, the rural vote turned thumbs down very decisively on Thomas Dewey in 1948. Neither in ideas nor personality did he match the rugged standards of those who prefer to work and live as individuals in the open country or in villages. But when Eisenhower ran, the rural Republican vote increased three and a half times. Even so, 50 per cent more country voters than big-city voters stayed home in 1952. Many, perhaps most, of them would have gotten out for a Senator Taft or a Senator Goldwater.

By deciding whether or not to vote, ruralites may well elect the president in 1964. For, according to the census, about 37 per cent of the population live in the open country or in places of less than 2,500. Only a fraction of these are farmers. Some of the others are ranchers, miners, lumbermen. Most, however, earn their income in some form of manufacturing or service, or else are retired—enabled to live at a considerable distance from their source of income by the automobile. While the farm population is declining, the rural nonfarm population may be growing faster even than the cities. In 1960, there were as many rural dwellers as persons in cities of over 500,000.

In many ways, of course, the country man and the urbanite are at opposite poles. The big city is the home of liberalism; the country, the source of conservatism. But as the 1960s wear on, with deep-seated problems over civil rights, the advance of automation, crime and bossism, and the encroachment of world communism, doubts are beginning to appear about the depth of the highly touted liberalism of the cities. In fact, it is becoming noticeable that the actions and apparent thinking of city dwellers, when faced with really big problems, are likely to be closer to those of the conservative country man than to his own words and professed ideology.

In the postmodern era, on no other basis than a true conception of human nature, can old and young, country man and city man, be united. Similarly, while the three sections into which the nation has traditionally been divided (West, South, and East) may still have somewhat different points of view on many questions, on the stark necessity of men behaving like human beings rather than like frolicking ideas out of the liberals' "Utopia Case Book," they can solidly unite. Conservatives in all sections and in all groups see our most pressing need today from basically the same point of view. Tariffs, free silver, trust-busting, labor unions, regulatory and even economic action by the government when necessary, a role of world leadership for the United States —these and other generalized issues have completely, or all but completely, passed out of partisan politics. And those who were on either side now find themselves united against the common foe: the extreme liberalism of today, which asserts that the very elements of a man's life that make him most unmistakably a man should be lived for him by the government—or by a machine.

One of the authors of this book (Paul Sexson) was secretary to former President Herbert Hoover when he was writing *The Challenge to Liberty*. Mr. Hoover said to him: "When there is a head-on collision between these two philosophies of government [conservatism and liberalism], there will be no doubt about how the American people will vote."

We agree.